A TASTE OF
SINGAPORE

A TASTE OF
SINGAPORE

Explore the sensational food and cooking of this unique cuisine, with 80 recipes shown step by step in more than 450 stunning photographs

Includes all the classic dishes, from Crab Curry and Lemon Chicken to Steamed Ginger and Coconut Milk Custards

Ghillie Başan and Terry Tan

southwater

This edition is published by Southwater,
an imprint of Anness Publishing Ltd, Blaby Road, Wigston,
Leicestershire LE18 4SE; info@anness.com

www.southwaterbooks.com; www.annesspublishing.com

If you like the images in this book and would like to investigate
using them for publishing, promotions or advertising, please visit
our website www.practicalpictures.com for more information.

Publisher: Joanna Lorenz
Editorial Director: Helen Sudell
Project Editors: Rosie Gordon and Elizabeth Young
Contributing Editor: Beverley Jollands
Home Economists: Lucy McKelvie, Bridget Sargeson
  and Fergal Connolly
Stylist: Helen Trent
Page Design: Mike Morey
Production Controller: Christine Ni

© Anness Publishing Ltd 2012

Previously published as part of a larger volume, *Classic Recipes,
Tastes and Traditions of Malaysia and Singapore*

Publisher's Note

Notes

Bracketed terms are intended for American readers.

For all recipes, quantities are given in both metric and imperial
measures and, where appropriate, in standard cups and
spoons. Follow one set of measures, but not a mixture,
because they are not interchangeable.

Standard spoon and cup measures are level.
1 tsp = 5ml, 1 tbsp = 15ml, 1 cup = 250ml/8fl oz.

Australian standard tablespoons are 20ml.
Australian readers should use 3 tsp in place of 1 tbsp for
measuring small quantities.

American pints are 16fl oz/2 cups.
American readers should use 20fl oz/2.5 cups in place of
1 pint when measuring liquids.

Electric oven temperatures in this book are for conventional
ovens. When using a fan oven, the temperature will probably
need to be reduced by about 10–20°C/20–40°F. Since ovens
vary, you should check with your manufacturer's instruction
book for guidance.

The nutritional analysis given for each recipe is calculated per
portion (i.e. serving or item), unless otherwise stated. If the
recipe gives a range, such as Serves 4–6, then the nutritional
analysis will be for the smaller portion size, i.e. 6 servings. The
analysis does not include optional ingredients, such as salt
added to taste.

Medium (US large) eggs are used unless otherwise stated.

Main front cover image shows Onion Pancakes – for recipe,
see page 63

Publisher's Acknowledgments

The publisher would like to thank William Lingwood and Martin
Brigdale for their photography throughout the book, apart from
the following images: Arcangel Images page 8; Photoshot
pp. 8b, 14, 39t.

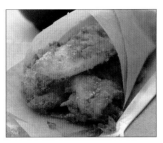

CONTENTS

INTRODUCTION

Often referred to as the "Manhattan of the East", Singapore is a consumer's paradise, and food is a national obsession. Everywhere you go there is something to eat and everywhere you look people are eating. Singapore is rich in diverse cultures and food traditions, but to many Singaporeans the origin of the dish is unimportant as long as it is tasty. Chinese food dominates, followed closely by Malay and Indian.

Most fascinating of all is how the culinary culture of Singapore has evolved. With no agriculture, but a great deal of affluence so that all manner of goods can be imported, the cuisine of the tiny nation has developed from the humble barrow on the street corner, selling one simple dish cooked on a single burner, to some of the most sophisticated hawker stalls in the world. For those who wish to dine in style, the Singapore restaurant scene ranks with the best in Sydney, Paris and New York, as the chefs are always creating new recipes and fusions.

The hawker tradition and coffee shop culture are most popular in Singapore, as many people are busy and live in tiny apartments, so eating out is the obvious choice. For some, cooking at home is only a weekend activity. High-class, air-conditioned food courts with tables and chairs are located in shopping malls and at the foot of office buildings. Food halls offer a truly multicultural culinary mix, as adjacent hawker stalls enable diners to taste a bit of Indian, Chinese and Malay at the same meal. But some locals argue that the most authentic food is still to be found at the little stalls on wheels clustered outside markets and coffee shops or by the roadside in more rural areas.

THE IMPORTANCE OF SPICE

Blending spice and seasonings is an art that has evolved through centuries of multiculturalism, and is today integral to the food. Singaporeans have endlessly adventurous tastebuds and experimentation is vital to their

Above: Noodle soups are very popular in Singapore. They are sold at hawker stalls and in coffee shops.

kitchens. The keynote of the cuisine is spice paste, pounded rough or smooth, fried or boiled, rubbed on seafood or meat; each cook does his own fine-tuning to produce dishes of delectable character and taste. Within the Chinese communities, many dishes of the Cantonese, Hakka and Fujian – the three migrant mainstreams from South China – have retained their intrinsic purity, but some have mutated deliciously to embrace the spicy spectrum. A Fujian soy braised duck is touched with coriander and pepper, a Cantonese noodle dish is liberally spiced up with Indian chilli paste, and Malay desserts are given a fragrant fillip with sesame seeds.

The subtle or robust flavours of Chinese stir-fries take on piquant highlights; for example, Chinese chicken dishes may be perfumed with indigenous herbs such as coriander (cilantro) and lemon grass. Coconut milk – the dairy equivalent in the region – is the liquid basis for many a hybrid creation, reflecting Indonesian, Thai and Indian culinary touches.

Left: Street stores sell an array of fruits, vegetables, fish, meat and much more, in Singapore's vibrant China Town.

Right: Singapore is an island city-state at the southern tip of West Malaysia (the Malay Peninsula).

A COOK'S HAVEN

In Singapore, tantalizing aromas fragrance the region's air, the coastal areas are teeming with marine life and there has always been an abundance of seafood and river catches. The reputation for incomparable culinary skills among Singaporean cooks – both professional and domestic – has been inherited by the people from their ingenious and inventive ancestors. Successive generations have adapted, improved and refined dishes, creating a rainbow palette of flavours. Of all the world's cuisines, these are some of the least intimidating, yet the most rewarding. Despite their complex flavours, basic cooks can prepare most dishes. There is no need for specialist equipment, as most dishes are derived from traditional and homely recipes across the cultures. Also, no two cooks ever interpret a recipe exactly the same way: ethnic cuisines have evolved over a long period of time and are never an exact science. Every cook or chef, new or established, has free licence to adapt a dish to suit the tastes of his family, community or customers.

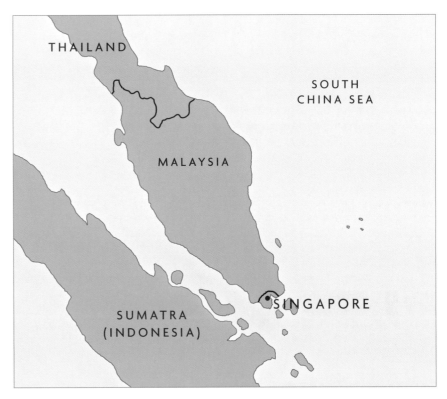

NONYA CUISINE

When the early Chinese traders began to settle in the ports of Penang, Melaka and Singapore from the 15th century onward, a number of them married local Malay women to create an ethnic sub-group of Malay-Chinese. In Malay, this group is called Peranakan, which means "half caste", but they also refer to themselves as Straits Chinese to distinguish themselves from the Chinese immigrant workers who came to the Malay Peninsula later.

Using the Peranakan words for male (*baba*) and female (*nonya*), this group was also referred to as the Baba-Nonyas, and was noted for its distinctive dress, lavishly decorated homes and, above all, its cuisine. The Peranakans were relatively wealthy, so they were able to indulge in elaborate meals that were an inspired mix of Chinese and Malay traditions. As the food was prepared by the women, it became known as Nonya cuisine.

To this day, the unique Nonya cooking is highly praised and much sought after, with its lavish use of chillies, lemon grass, galangal and turmeric fused with elements of Indian, Thai, Portuguese and Chinese cooking methods. Classic Nonya dishes include *mee siam*, a Thai-influenced dish of rice noodles in a spicy, tangy sauce, and *babi pong tey*, a pork stew cooked in an earthenware pot.

Below: Satay dishes can include every form of fish, meat and vegetable.

Below: Warm custards make for a deliciously sweet mid-afternoon treat.

TRADITIONAL FOOD IN MODERN LIFE

In Singapore, the pace of life is fast and urban. The population is 76 per cent Chinese, 15 per cent Malay and 6 per cent Indian, with a small number of Peranakan, Eurasian and Indonesian, sprinkled with Western influences. This all adds up to one of the most colourful and exciting culinary scenes in the world, made all the more tangible by the fascinating tradition of hawker stalls, where exotic food from all these cultures can be sampled in one place.

Living in a highly urbanized city state, Singaporeans have, over several decades, nurtured the love of food to a passionate degree, even though every ingredient is imported from somewhere else. You can scarcely move 50 metres before you come across yet another food court or hawker centre that offers the aromatic promise of dishes from a dozen different regions.

Above: Singapore City is vibrant and colourful, like its cuisine.

Right: Customers waiting to be served at a street stall in Singapore selling Hainanese specialities.

FOOD TO GO

Muslim and Malay stalls are often grouped together, selling *sop kambing* (Indian-inspired mutton soup), *mee siam* (Thai-influenced spicy tangy noodles) and *bubur* (traditional Malay rice porridge), served with side dishes such as fried anchovies. At grill stalls you will find spicy chicken wings, stingray wings served in banana leaves, and fish, beef, chicken or lamb satay. Rice stalls may offer a selection of dishes or just one with their rice.

Cze cha stalls generally display a mix of Chinese and Malay snacks, such as noodles in broth, fish balls, stuffed chillies and dumplings, while noodle stalls lure you with the sweet, spicy aromas of stir-fried shellfish, ginger and garlic. Rice cake stalls serve these South Indian specialities, with chutneys and sambals, for breakfast or a mid-morning snack, and the *roti* stalls specialize in more Indian staples such as flatbreads and various *dhals*.

Sweet stalls offer Malay, Chinese, Indian and Peranakan snacks and desserts, such as *gulab jamun*, the Indian deep-fried sweetmeats made with coconut milk; *kueh-kueh*, which are Peranakan tea cakes; and Chinese sweet bean soups. Ice cream is also popular, and is sold from stalls and small refrigerators attached to bicycles.

Seasonal fruits are displayed at fruit and juice stalls and can be bought in wedges or blended into a drink. Snack stalls sell roasted chestnuts; salted or sugared *kacang*, which is a mixture of roasted peanuts, peas and beans; deep-fried prawn (shrimp) crackers; deep-fried bananas and *vadai* (dhal fritters).

As Singapore is divided into racial quarters, the hawker stalls and coffee shops follow a similar pattern. In Katong, the Peranakan and Eurasian section, they offer competitive versions of Singapore *laksa* (noodles in coconut milk) right next to coffee shops selling European tea cakes or Chinese chicken rice cafés. In Little India, the warm,

spicy aromas of the Tekka Market attract Hindu, Muslim and Chinese shoppers, as well as the Nonyas (Peranakan ladies) and European *taitais* (ladies of leisure) who descend on the Indian coffee shops to tuck into a freshly made *roti paratha* (flaky flatbread), with sweet pulled tea.

The *dosai* shops sell Indian rice crêpes and vegetarian dishes, as they are run by Hindus who do not eat meat. In the same areas you will find Indian "banana leaf" restaurants, where the food is served on banana leaves.

Some dishes are unique to Singapore – they may be versions of traditional dishes from elsewhere that have been given a Singapore twist, or new creations by adventurous chefs. One that has become a classic is stir-fried chilli crab in a tomato sauce, which is invariably eaten with the fingers and mopped up with a French baguette.

MARKETPLACES

The markets represent the fabulous reality of Singapore's integrated multiculturalism and culinary fusion, with a breathtaking volume and variety of local produce as well as imported fruits and vegetables, which are all vociferously haggled over. A typical market has wet and dry regions, divided into rows to separate meat from fish, vegetables from fruit, and dried beans and grains from condiments. At the edges, there are stalls selling pots and pans, brooms and mops, clothes and shoes, and makeshift food stalls selling snacks, fruit and drinks. Sweet iced coffee is popular, and busy workers rely on a crude version of "carry-out" coffee, served in cleaned-out condensed milk cans. The large central markets stay open all day, the local neighbourhood ones close at midday, and the open-air night markets close around midnight, creating a lovely evening throng.

ABOUT THIS BOOK

Perhaps you have visited Singapore and long to relive the tastes and scents of the food you ate there, or have enjoyed a Singaporean meal in a restaurant. Alternatively, you may enjoy Malaysian, Thai or Indian food and want to discover related cuisines. Whatever the case, you will find here a superb collection of recipes that showcase the best of Singaporean cuisine.

In the section about ingredients, there is useful information on how to prepare foods in an authentic way. Many of the ingredients featured may be unfamiliar to Western cooks, but this discovery of exotic vegetables and fruits, beautiful fish and pungent spices is part of the fascination of learning to cook food from other areas of the world.

The recipes aim to immerse you in the true experience of Singapore's food, with classic soups, street food and snacks, noodle and rice dishes, exotic desserts, and meat and seafood dishes with incomparable flavour.

These dishes make the most of fresh ingredients, as well as regional store-cupboard staples, and are easy to prepare quickly and enjoy.

How eateries have changed

Eating is a passion in Singapore, a national pastime quite simply because there's so much food and it's so good. Since Singapore's founding in 1819 by Englishman Stamford Raffles, its cooking has been a delicious amalgam of Chinese, British Colonial, Malay, Arab, Thai, Indian, Indonesian and European food elements.

Until the mid-1980s, hawkers plied their wares in makeshift carts, but government regulations and Singapore's massive urbanization programme then dictated that hawker stalls must be contained within purpose-built food courts. They are no longer termed hawkers, and have been relocated to covered complexes dotting the island. The flavours of street food still abound, but the ambience is more pristine than rustic. Many are air-conditioned with impeccable hygiene standards while others are relaxed, but all are in keeping with strict government health regulations.

One can still dine on a mélange of dishes when along the East Coast or within the plush comfort of five-star coffee-houses, purpose-built complexes in department stores and updated terraced shophouses. Obviously all this is reflected in the prices, though these, while higher than they used to be, are still affordable for most Singaporeans. The food itself has remained largely unchanged. The template for the food courts remains multicultural, a delicious gathering of many different cuisines under one roof. Most open until late at night, offering cheap and delicious ethnic dishes of every type.

Most of the dishes are those that evolved from the original hawkers. They are suited to mass catering and often call for fairly complex preparation, which householders are not inclined to do after a hard day's work. Many dishes require stir-frying in huge woks over roaring fires, which few homes have. It has become something of a national practice to stop by for dinner after work, or to buy cartons to take home.

Right: A statue of Sir Stamford Raffles in Singapore City reminds visitors of the city's colonial past.

EQUIPMENT, TECHNIQUES AND INGREDIENTS

The culinary cultures of Singapore have been greatly influenced by the cuisines of Malaysia, India, Thailand, China and Eurasia, so there are inevitably many similarities. The following pages introduce both fresh ingredients and processed foods, discussing their aroma, taste, texture and appearance, and describing essential preparation and cooking techniques.

EQUIPMENT

The traditional South-east Asian kitchen is basic. Often dark and sparsely kitted out with an open hearth, very little equipment is needed. Food is generally bought daily from the markets, taken home and cooked immediately, so unless you visit the kitchen during the frenzied moments of activity over the hearth, there is little evidence of food or cooking in homes.

In the days when there were no refrigerators, the reliance on fresh produce from the daily markets was vital. For some, two visits to the market were required – in the morning for the ingredients to cook for lunch, and in the afternoon for the evening meal.

Back in the kitchen, the activity begins with the scrubbing of vegetables, the plucking and jointing of birds (if it hasn't been done in the markets), endless chopping and slicing, and the pounding of herbs and spices with a mortar and pestle.

WOK

The wok is the most important utensil for everyday cooking and everybody has one. Without a doubt, there is always something delicious being stir-fried in a home or in the streets. However, woks are not only used for stir-frying, they are also used for steaming, deep-frying, braising and soup-making. The most functional, multi-purpose wok should measure approximately 35cm/14in across, large enough for a family meal or to steam a whole fish. The most common wok is double-handled and made of lightweight carbonized steel. This is ideal for deep-frying and steaming but, for stir-frying, you need the single-handled version.

When you first buy a wok, you need to season it before use. Put it over a high heat to blacken the inside – this burns off any dust and factory coating. Leave the wok to cool, then immerse it in hot, soapy water and clean it with an abrasive cloth or stiff brush. Rinse it well and dry over a medium heat. Pour a little cooking oil into the base and, using kitchen paper, wipe all around the surface of the wok. Now the wok is ready for use.

After each use, clean the wok with hot water only, dry it over a medium heat, and wipe a thin layer of oil over the surface. This will ensure that it doesn't get rusty.

Above: A solid mortar and pestle is an essential piece of kitchen equipment.

MORTAR AND PESTLE

A big mortar and pestle, made of stone, is of particular value, as it is used not only for grinding spices, chillies and garlic, but also for pounding all the condiments and pastes, as well as the meat for pâtés and savoury balls. Some cooks have several mortar and pestle sets, varying in size according to the activity and ingredient. Coffee grinders and electric blenders can be used as substitutes, but they don't release the oils and flavours of the ingredients in the same way and they produce too smooth a texture. It is worth looking for a solid stone mortar and pestle in Asian markets and kitchen suppliers.

BAMBOO STEAMER

Traditional bamboo steamers come in various sizes. The most practical one is about 30cm/12in wide, as it can be used for rice or a whole fish. Generally, the steamer is set directly over a wok that is filled with boiling water to below the level of the steamer. The food is placed in the steamer, either on a plate, or wrapped in muslin (cheesecloth), or banana leaves. The lid is placed on the steamer and, as the water in the wok is heated, the steam rises under and around the food, cooking it gently. A stainless steel steamer is no substitute for a bamboo one, which imparts its

Left: A single-handled wok is good for stir-frying; a double-handled wok is better for steaming and deep-frying.

own delicate fragrance to the dish. Bamboo steamers are available in most Asian stores and some cooking equipment suppliers.

CHOPSTICKS

For cooking, look for long chopsticks made from bamboo. Chopsticks are used to eat with, as well as for cooking, and many cooks will use a set of long chopsticks for stirring, mixing, tasting, and as tongs. Eating chopsticks are traditionally made from bamboo or wood, but more elaborate ones can be made from ivory, bone, gold, silver or jade.

CLAY POT

Made from a combination of light-coloured clay and sand, these pots come in all sizes, with single or double handles, lids, and glazed interiors. Perhaps the oldest form of cooking

Right: Bamboo steamers come in several sizes.

vessel, these attractive pots are ideal for slow-cooking, braised dishes and soups, as they retain an overall even heat. Generally, they are used on the stove over a low or medium heat, as a high temperature could cause a crack. When you first buy a clay pot, it needs to be treated for cooking. Fill it with water and place it over a low flame, then gradually increase the heat and let the water boil until it is reduced by half. Rinse the pot and dry it thoroughly. Now it is ready for use. Traditional clay pots are available in some Asian markets.

Above: A clay pot can be used in the oven or, with care, on the stove.

Below: Bamboo chopsticks are essential kitchen equipment.

*Above:
A medium-weight cleaver is a multi-purpose tool.*

CLEAVERS

Asian cleavers are the most important tools in the kitchen. There are special blades for the fine chopping of lemon grass and green papaya, heavy blades for opening coconuts, thin ones for shredding spring onions (scallions), and multi-purpose ones for any type of chopping, slicing and crushing. Generally, you use the front, lighter part of the blade for the regular chopping, slicing and shredding; the back, heavier section is for chopping with force through bones; and the flat side is ideal for crushing ginger and garlic, and for transporting ingredients into the wok.

DRAINING SPOONS

Traditional draining spoons are made of wire and have a long bamboo handle; more modern ones are made completely of stainless steel with a perforated spoon. Both are flat and extremely useful for deep-frying, for blanching noodles and for scooping ingredients out of any hot liquid.

Above: Draining spoons are useful for deep-frying and blanching.

COOKING TECHNIQUES

The traditional cooking methods of Singapore require few culinary tools but a great deal of attention to detail. Fresh ingredients are of the utmost importance, followed by the balance of sharp or mild, salty or sweet, bitter or sour, or a combination of all of these flavours. The layering of ingredients is also important, especially in noodle dishes, where flavours and textures should complement each other but remain separate.

Many meals are prepared from scratch, starting with the plucking of chickens and grinding of spices, followed by grilling over charcoal, gentle simmering and steaming, or stir-frying. Armed with the correct equipment, the cooking is easy – most of the work, and the key to culinary success, is in the preparation.

STEAMING

This is a popular way of preparing delicate-tasting foods, such as fish and shellfish, pork-filled dumplings and sticky rice cakes wrapped in bamboo or banana leaves. Place the food in a bamboo steamer, which should be lined with leaves if the food isn't wrapped in them. Put the lid on the steamer and set it over a wok that is half-filled with water. Bring the water to the boil, then reduce the heat and steam the food according to the recipe.

Above: Fish wrapped in banana leaves with spices steams to perfumed perfection on a bamboo rack.

DRY-FRYING

Dried spices are often roasted before grinding to release their natural oils and enhance the aroma.

1 Spread the spices thinly in a wok or heavy pan and put it over a high heat.

2 As the pan begins to heat, shake it so that the spices don't get too brown.

3 Once the spices begin to colour and their aroma fills the air, put them in a mortar and grind to a powder.

BRAISING

The classic slow-cooking method is braising. Oily fish, duck and red meat are often cooked this way, with herbs, spices and coconut milk or juice.

Traditionally, to seal in the moisture, a covered clay pot is used. Placed over a medium heat, or in the oven, cooking can take from 30 minutes to 2 hours, depending on the dish. If you don't have a clay pot, use a heavy-based casserole. The key is in containing the moisture and even heat distribution, so don't use a thin aluminium pot.
Simply put all the ingredients in a clay pot and place in a preheated oven. (It can also be placed over a medium heat on the stove if you prefer.)

GRILLING OVER CHARCOAL

As conventional grills (broilers) don't exist in most homes in South-east Asia, grilling is generally done outdoors over hot charcoal.

This traditional method of cooking not only lends itself to many types of food, it also enhances the taste. Whole fish, pigs or chickens can be cooked this way. Tasty, marinated morsels of food, skewered on bamboo sticks and grilled in the streets, make popular snacks. When cooking over charcoal, light the coals and wait until they are covered with grey or white ashes. If the charcoal is too hot, the food will just burn.

Wooden and bamboo skewers
If you are using wooden or bamboo skewers, soak them in water for about 30 minutes before using to prevent them from burning.

STIR-FRYING

Of all the cooking techniques, this is the most important one in Singapore. The technique is more in the preparation of ingredients than in the cooking process, which takes only minutes. Generally, the ingredients should be cut or shredded into bitesize morsels and laid out in the order in which they are to be cooked. To stir-fry successfully you need a wok, placed over a high heat, and a ladle or spatula to toss the ingredients around, so that they cook but still retain their freshness and crunchy texture.

In stir frying, the key is to work quickly and layer the ingredients according to the length of time they require for cooking. Serve the dish hot straight from the wok into warmed bowls and don't leave the food sitting in the wok – it must be enjoyed fresh.

1 Pour a little oil into the wok and place it over a high heat until hot.

2 Add the spices and aromatics to the oil – it should sizzle on contact – and toss them around to flavour the oil. It is important to keep stirring quickly in order to move the ingredients around the wok and ensure that they do not burn. They will release plenty of aroma.

3 Add the pieces of meat or fish, and toss them in the wok for two minutes.

4 Add the sliced firm vegetables or mushrooms and stir-fry for a minute.

5 Add the leafy vegetables or bean-sprouts and toss them around quickly.

6 Finally, toss in the herbs, seasonings or sauce, mix well and serve piping hot.

DEEP-FRYING

Use an oil that can be heated to a high temperature, such as groundnut (peanut) oil, and don't put in too much cold food at once, as this will cool the oil down.

1 Pour the oil into a wok or pan (filling it no more than two-thirds full) and heat to about 180°C/350°F. To test the temperature, add a drop of batter or a piece of onion. If it sinks, the oil is not hot enough; if it burns, it is too hot. If it sizzles and rises to the surface, the temperature is perfect.

2 Cook the food in small batches until crisp and lift out with a slotted spoon or wire mesh skimmer when cooked. Drain on a wire rack lined with kitchen paper and serve immediately, or keep warm in the oven until ready to serve.

BLANCHING

This method is often used to cook delicate meat such as chicken breast portions or duck.

Place the meat and any flavourings in a pan and add just enough water to cover. Bring to the boil, then remove from the heat and leave to stand, covered, for 10 minutes, then drain.

RICE

Rice has been a staple crop throughout most of tropical Asia for many generations, and it is around a communal bowl of comfortingly hot, fluffy white rice that most meals are built. Rich in carbohydrate and containing vitamins A and B, rice is one of the healthiest grains. From it comes rice vinegar and rice wine, which are also indispensable to Chinese cooking, which influences dishes in Singapore and throughout South-east Asia. Ground rice flour is made into rice noodles, *dim sum* dumpling skins, and a wide range of sweet puddings.

For good reason, rice is regarded as the "staff of life" and some superstitions connected to its power still hold sway. In every rice-eating household, there is invariably a large barrel or tin in which the raw rice is stored. This must never be completely emptied as it is bad feng shui. As the last few grains are reached families hurriedly top the container up to the brim for fear of attracting bad luck or negative energy. In "rice bowl" areas such as the north Malaysian state of Kedah, rice agriculture is bound up with reverent rites and near mystical rituals, in which offerings are made to the rice deity.

In times past, freshly harvested rice was pounded in an enormous pestle and mortar and then winnowed to

Below: A Malaysian farmer harvests his rice crop.

remove the husk and bran before it could be cooked. Commercial milling of rice began in the mid-19th century. Singapore has virtually no agricultural land and rice has never been grown here to any extent.

All meals are communal, built around rice, and the colloquial greeting among older people is "Have you eaten rice?" which is the equivalent of asking "How are you?" It truly reflects the reverence in which the grain is held. Be it a Chinese, Malay, Peranakan or Indian meal, rice is on the menu.

RICE DISHES

There are only two methods of cooking rice: boiling and steaming. But the precious grain is by no means confined to being boiled and eaten unadorned. Once cooked thus, it can be used as the basis of many other dishes. Indian cooking especially has elevated rice to delicious heights, matched by few others for spicy ingenuity. Rice with saffron, turmeric, ghee and mustard oil, enriched with nuts and seeds, is translated into glorious pilaffs.

Within the Chinese kitchen, rice receives much the same reverence, and special *yang chao* fried rice has become a global culinary favourite. Jasmine rice, also called Thai fragrant rice, is grown widely in China, Malaysia, Thailand and Indonesia and forms the basis of most Chinese and Malay rice dishes in Singapore. Good quality jasmine rice

Above: Jasmine or Thai fragrant rice has tender, aromatic grains. It is widely available in supermarkets in the West.

has a subtly delicate scent, with dry, thin and firm grains that are translucent when raw. Boiled or steamed, the texture should be firm and still retain some bite. The colour should be a pristine white and when you rake it with a fork, it should fluff up nicely.

LONG GRAIN RICE

Basmati has the longest grain of all in proportion to its size, and peculiarly the grains become longer and not wider when cooked. Long grain and Basmati rice are indigenous to India and Pakistan and are grown mainly in the Punjab. They are ideal for many humble or grand Muglai dishes.

Basmati rice has a distinctive, nutty flavour and is popular among Singapore Indians for cooking their beloved biryanis. It is also becoming increasingly popular with Chinese cooks, as the longer, denser grains lend themselves to frying without clumping together. Both Basmati and American long grain are far less sticky than short grain rice.

SHORT GRAIN RICE

Chinese Teochew families eat a traditional meal called Teochew *mui*, or *congee*, which is made using short grain rice cooked until it resembles porridge, with a lot of milky liquid that is reputed to settle the stomach. *Congee* is served with a wide range of pickles, stir fries and simple dishes.

GLUTINOUS RICE

All types of rice contain a certain amount of starch, though all are gluten free. The varieties imported from Thailand and Laos, whether long grain or jasmine, tend to contain relatively high levels; hence the produce of these regions is known as "sticky rice" or "glutinous rice". There are two kinds of starch in any cereal grain: amylopectin and amylase. Sticky rice is high in amylopectin, and when the rice is cooked, these molecules form a gel, enclosing water within their strands.

Glutinous rice accounts for less than 2 per cent of world output and it is used mainly in desserts, although it is often eaten in tandem with normal rice. Preference for this rice here is very likely due to the influence of Thai immigrants.

Glutinous rice comes in both long and short grain varieties. The grains have to be soaked for several hours, sometimes overnight, before cooking. For festive dishes such as saffron or turmeric rice for weddings, it is turned out as savoury offerings, often perfumed with rose water, cinnamon and cloves. It is rarely boiled and eaten plain as part of a meal unless for a special occasion such as the Nonya Long Table feast. Glutinous rice mainly lends itself to the making of dumplings, puddings and festive sweets.

In contrast to normal long grain rice, the highly polished, glutinous rice grain is an opaque white colour when raw, and turns translucent when cooked. Although the texture of cooked glutinous rice is quite firm, it is nevertheless sticky and clumps together like a lump of dough. It is this characteristic that makes it popular as a wraparound for a range of filled rice dishes. During the Chinese Dragon Boat festival, also called the Dumpling Festival, triangular dumplings are made with glutinous rice encasing spicy meat or mung bean paste. They are boiled for several hours and eaten as a snack.

Above: Black and white glutinous rice.

BLACK GLUTINOUS RICE

This unpolished, wholegrain glutinous rice is almost exclusively used for sweet dishes. When soaked in water and cooked, the grains turn a deep reddish-purple. In Singapore, black sticky rice is called *pulut hitam*, and in the Nonya dessert of the same name it is served with coconut cream and palm sugar. It must be soaked for several hours or overnight before cooking. Black sticky rice is available in some Asian markets.

Above: Patna rice is one of the many types of long-grain rice.

RICE PRODUCTS

There are many rice products that you will begin to use when you get familiar with the food of Singapore and widen your repertoire.

Ground rice or rice flour

Used in making all kinds of sticky sweets and cakes, such as the Teochew *mua chee* (from which the Japanese derive *mochi*), ground rice is also a thickener for soups and stews. It is mixed with self-raising (self-rising) flour in a batter for banana and sweet potato fritters, which are favourite Singapore snacks. Rice flour is made by grinding the raw grain until it is very fine. All rice grains can be used and the packets are usually labelled accordingly. Long grain and medium grain rice flour is used to make dough for fresh and dried rice noodles, as well as for dumplings, crêpes and buns.

Glutinous rice flour, sometimes called sweet rice flour, is reserved for sweet pastries, pancakes and cakes. Do not confuse this with rice powder, which is much finer ground rice and is used in delicate bakes. Both types are available from Asian stores and should be kept in an airtight container in a dry place.

Rice papers

A large community of Chinese settled in South Vietnam several centuries ago and they still keep to their classical cuisine while adapting many indigenous dishes, and these practices tend to spread. Originally unique to Thai and Vietnamese cuisines, triangular or circular rice papers and wrappers have been adopted by Chinese chefs around the world. Rice papers are spreading in popularity, and are now used in Singapore as a delicate skin for spring rolls. Once deep fried, they make an extremely thin and crispy case.

Made from rice flour, water and salt, "raw" rice papers are brittle. They need to be soaked briefly in hot water until they are soft and pliant. When each wrapper has softened, lift it out of the water with a chopstick and spread it on a chopping board before topping with filling. Once rolled up, the packets can be eaten as they are or deep-fried. If you are deep frying them do so in small batches, as the delicate wrappers are liable to stick together and break open in a crowded fryer or wok.

Packets of dried rice papers are available in Asian stores and some supermarkets. Do not confuse them with the sheets of rice paper used in baking.

Above and right: Amber and white rice vinegar have a distinctive sharpness.

Above: Rice papers are dried on bamboo mats, which give them their familiar cross-hatch pattern.

Rice wine and vinegar

Throughout China, rice is distilled to make wine and vinegar. The grains are fermented in a process similar to making beer, to produce a highly alcoholic brew. The resulting clear, clean-tasting vinegar is used extensively in Singapore, especially among the Chinese populations, who prefer it to normal vinegar as it has a delicious aroma and is less acidic. Red rice is used to make a distinctive red wine vinegar that is an essential seasoning for northern Chinese casseroles. Black rice vinegar is usually made from black glutinous rice, and is sweet and smoky in flavour. Bottles of rice wine and vinegar are available in Asian and Chinese stores and markets.

PREPARING AND COOKING RICE

Many people find difficulty in preparing soft, fluffy rice. You may get varying advice about this depending on where you are, but there are actually few fundamental rules. Most rice grains are cooked using the absorption method, except glutinous rice, which is soaked and steamed.

Washing rice

In most Asian countries, raw rice is washed several times – traditionalists will insist that it goes through "seven changes of water" but this has more to do with myth than common sense. Most of the rice bought in supermarkets today requires minimal washing to remove traces of husks or discoloured grains. However, long grain rice does benefit from rinsing in cold water to reduce the excess starch, so that the cooked grains are light and fluffy and separate easily.

1 Put the measured quantity of grains into a bowl and cover with cold water. Swirl the grains in the water until it becomes cloudy, then leave to settle.

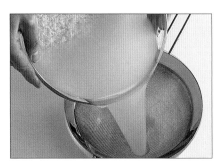

2 Strain the rice through a sieve (strainer) then return it to the bowl and repeat until the water is clear.

Soaking

Some culinary institutes teach trainee chefs to soak rice before cooking. There are two reasons for this. Soaking is said to bleach the rice so that, when cooked, the colour is more intensely white. The other reason is that increasing the moisture content of the grains in this way means that the cooking water can penetrate more effectively. Consequently the grains are less likely to break up and stickiness is reduced, resulting in fluffier rice.

After rinsing the rice, leave the grains in the bowl and cover with cold water. Leave to soak for half an hour. Drain the rice through a sieve (strainer), rinse it under cold running water, then drain again before you cook it.

Steaming

Rice that is to be steamed needs only the minimum amount of water – just covering it – and it should be steamed in a flat vessel such as a shallow pan or a traditional bamboo steamer. Cover the rice to keep in the steam.

Test if the rice is cooked by eating a few grains. There should be a slight resistance to the bite.

1 Fill a wok one-third full with water. Place a bamboo steamer, with the lid on, over the wok and bring the water underneath to the boil.

2 Lift the lid off the steamer and place a dampened piece of clean muslin (cheesecloth) over the rack. Put the rice in the middle and spread it out a little. Fold the edges of the muslin over the rice, put the lid back on the steamer and steam for about 25 minutes, until the rice is tender but still firm.

Cooking by absorption

Rice soaks up a lot of water as it cooks – 450g/1lb of uncooked rice will absorb up to 600ml/1 pint of water, making enough to feed four moderate appetites (though probably only two hungry labourers). The volume of rice grains doubles when cooked.

The proportion of water required and the cooking time will both vary slightly with different grains, so it is wise to follow the instructions on the packet if you are cooking an unusual variety of rice. Put the measured grains into a heavy pan with a proportionally measured amount of water, and cook the rice until all the water has been absorbed. The age-old method for judging the amount of water is to add enough to come up to two joints of the index finger from the top of the rice.

1 Put the rinsed grains into a heavy pan and pour in the water. Bring to the boil, stir once, then reduce the heat to low.

2 Cover the pan tightly and leave to cook very gently for 15–20 minutes, depending on the size of the grain, until all the liquid has been absorbed. Remove the pan from the heat and leave to stand for 5–10 minutes to allow the residual heat to finish the cooking.

3 When the water is absorbed, fluff the tender rice up with a fork and serve.

Using an automatic rice cooker

Once the preserve of the Japanese, rice cookers are now practically universal and are one of the easiest and most trouble-free methods of cooking rice. Simply wash and drain the rice, place it in the inner cooker bowl with the requisite amount of water, and switch on. When the rice is cooked, it will switch itself off. The cooker works by weight, with the inner pot resting on a springboard. When all the water is absorbed, it switches off automatically as the lighter inner pot springs back to its original position.

Cooking in a microwave

Prepare the rice as for a rice cooker but you should not cover the pot as water will boil over and spill. For 250g/9oz rice you will need 300ml/½ pint water, though long grain rice may need more as it is a denser grain.

ADDITIONAL FLAVOURINGS

Generally, rice in Singapore is eaten plain, and is not salted or seasoned because it acts as a foil to the other flavours in the meal. However, Indian meals may feature rice perfumed with rose water, ghee or saffron to go with curries and sambals.

When coconut rice is called for, the grains are cooked in coconut milk and the rice is often served with fried anchovies, nuts and strips of omelette, and sometimes spiced up with a fiery chilli sambal. For weddings and festive occasions, cooks sometimes prepare a yellow coloured rice, which is flavoured and coloured a bright yellow with ground turmeric.

NOODLES

South-east Asian cooking uses noodles in great quantities. If the main dish doesn't contain rice it will consist of noodles. They are eaten at all hours of the day, in soup for breakfast, simply stir-fried for a filling snack, or incorporated into main dishes with meat, fish and vegetables. It is no wonder that most food stalls and hawker centres in Singapore serve both staples in many combinations.

Noodles are made from either rice or wheat flour, and the everyday noodles in Singapore fall into several main types. *Mee* or *mien* are made from wheat flour, sometimes with egg, and are either thin and long or flat, much like tagliatelle pasta strands. Wheat noodles come in a wide range of types, many from China, and are usually sold dried, in packets.

Rice noodles also come in a variety of shapes. Long, flat noodles are called *kway teow*, and thin versions are called *mi fun* or *bee hoon*. Singaporeans prefer to use fresh noodles if the dish calls for *kway teow*, but the thin variety is usually sold dry.

Noodle stalls are ubiquitous and the hundreds of food courts each have at least three or four noodle stalls. Noodles served with minced (ground) pork and fishball soup have become an iconic

Singapore dish, as has Singapore *laksa*, a rich, coconut milk-based noodle dish with lashings of chilli paste and aromatic laksa leaves.

FRESH RICE NOODLES

These are a mainstay among the Teochews who love them in a soup dish called *kway teow th'ng*. The Cantonese have a different use for the same type, known as *hor fun*, either uncooked or stir-fried with meat, seafood and vegetables; and fresh rice noodles are also used in the popular Singapore hawker dish of *char kway teow*.

Virtually every wet market and supermarket sells fresh rice noodles, supplied daily by local manufacturers. They are sometimes frozen but mainly chilled, in packets.

FINE RICE NOODLES

Commonly called rice vermicelli, there are several types of varying thicknesses, all sold dry. A favourite Fujian or Hokkien type called *mee sua* are extremely thin and delicate, and are usually reserved for special birthday dishes as they symbolize longevity. Another even less common type is called *mee teow*, and is used exclusively in Teochew dishes.

RICE STICKS

Though not in widespread use, dry rice sticks are useful because of their long shelf life. They are gradually becoming more popular among busy people who do not have time to buy the fresh variety daily. They are simply briefly boiled or blanched depending on the type. Generally much thinner than the fresh variety, they are ideal for soups but tend to break up easily when fried.

PREPARING RICE NOODLES

Virtually nobody in Singapore bothers to make their own fresh rice noodles because they are so widely available. However, they are worth the effort for special occasions. Fresh rice noodles need to be blanched briefly in hot water and drained before use in soups or stir-fries. Vermicelli, on the other hand, need only to be soaked for about 20 minutes.

Dried rice noodles double in bulk when rehydrated. Once prepared this way, they should not be cooked for too long or they turn mushy and break up. About 150g/5oz of reconstituted noodles are sufficient for one portion, as each bowl will also contain vegetables, meat or seafood.

Throughout the two countries rice noodle soup or fried noodles are daily fare. The added ingredients vary: pork, fish balls, prawns, vegetables, liver, kidneys and beef. Lamb is never used.

MAKING FRESH RICE NOODLES

A variety of dried noodles are available from Asian stores and supermarkets in the West, but fresh ones are quite different and if you want to make them yourself it's not that difficult. For a snack, freshly made noodle sheets can be drenched in sugar or honey, or dipped into a sweet or savoury sauce of your choice. Alternatively, you can cut them into wide strips and gently stir-fry them with garlic, ginger, chillies and *nuoc mam* or soy sauce – a popular snack enjoyed all over South-east Asia.

Left: Different types of dried rice and wheat noodles are used for soups, stir fries, salads and even sweet snacks.

As a guide, to serve four you will need about 225g/8oz/2 cups rice flour and 600ml/1pint/2½ cups water. You will also need a wide pot with a domed lid, or a wok lid, a piece of thin, smooth cotton cloth (such as an old clean sheet) and a lightly oiled baking tray.

Preparing the batter

Place the flour in a bowl and stir in a little water to form a smooth paste. Gradually pour in the rest of the water, whisking all the time to make sure there are no lumps. Beat in a pinch of salt and 15ml/1 tbsp vegetable oil. Set aside for 15 minutes.

Preparing the steamer

Meanwhile, fill a wide pot with water. Cut a piece of cloth a little larger than the top of the pot. Stretch it over the top of the pot (you may need someone to help you), pulling the edges down over the sides so that the cloth is as taut as a drum, then wind a piece of string around the edge, securing the cloth with a knot or bow. Using a sharp knife, make 3 small slits, about 2.5cm/1in from the edge of the cloth, at regular intervals. If you need to top up the water during cooking, pour it through these slits.

Cooking the noodle sheets

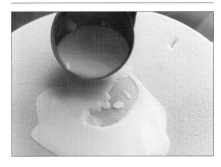

1 Bring the water in the pot to the boil. Once it is bubbling and steam is rising through the cloth, stir the batter and ladle a portion (roughly 30–45ml/2–3 tbsp) on to the cloth, swirling it to form a 10–15cm/4–6in wide circle.

2 Cover the pot with the domed lid and steam for 1 minute, until the noodle sheet is translucent. To remove it, carefully insert a spatula or round-bladed knife under the edge of the noodle sheet and gently prize it off the cloth – if it doesn't peel off easily, you may need to steam it for a little longer.

3 Transfer the sheet to the oiled tray and repeat with the rest of the batter. As they accumulate, stack the sheets on top of each other, brushing the tops with oil so they don't stick together. Cover the stack with a clean dish towel to keep them moist.

COOK'S TIP

During the cooking, you may have to top up the water through one of the slits. The cloth might occasionally need to be pulled tight again over the sides of the pot if it begins to sag, otherwise the batter will form a pool and the noodle sheets will be too thick in the centre.

MUNG BEAN NOODLES

Called by many names – transparent noodles, translucent vermicelli, cellophane or glass noodles – these are made from mung bean flour and are always sold dry. They reconstitute rapidly when soaked in warm water and have the peculiar characteristic that they keep their crunch no matter how long you cook them. Usually sold in small skeins, they have a neutral flavour that soaks up seasoning very well, and are often simply cooked in stock.

WHEAT FLOUR NOODLES

Generally pale yellow, these come either dried to be reconstituted or fresh to be blanched before use in stir-fries or curries. There are three distinct types: factory-produced dried skeins of yellow noodles that have to be boiled for a few minutes or longer depending on the type; freshly made and semi-dry noodles usually with a light coating of flour that need only to be blanched; and fresh yellow noodles that need very light cooking.

Some producers oil their fresh yellow noodles, and these must be blanched thoroughly to remove the grease. Dry noodles, like rice sticks and vermicelli, double in bulk when reconstituted but fresh ones remain the same.

Some wheat noodles contain egg and resemble Japanese udon. They are often referred to as Shanghai-style noodles, and are usually sold fresh. They are firmer and denser than rice noodles and are used in stir-fries and soups. Fairly new to the market is a variety infused with spinach, which colours the noodles pale green.

HAND-TOSSED NOODLES

A recent import from north China, these noodles are made fresh, more as a theatrical performance than to meet consumer demand. It takes years of practice before you can knead wheat flour into a firm but elastic dough, then pull and stretch it constantly until fine threads appear before your very eyes. Most restaurants that offer this dish charge a premium price, as only a limited amount can be made each day.

BREAD

The bread that is familiar in the West was not eaten by Singaporeans until the beginning of the British Colonial era in the early 19th century. Nevertheless, the loaf has been adopted and adapted as a part of meals since then. Neighbouring Vietnam and Cambodia had been colonized by the French, who introduced the baguette, but the former British colonies did not embrace the staple with the same passion until relatively recently.

Early Arab traders in Singapore already made their own Middle Eastern loaf and cooks employed by British army families were taught to make basic white loaves and baps. With the increased availability of imported products and baking skills, bread became more accepted. Bakeries began to thrive after World War II and bread became more available. Today, bakers in Singapore produce a wide range of Western-style breads.

BUNS, SANDWICHES AND TOASTS

Visitors to Singapore in the 1950s would have been surprised to find ice cream vendors selling slices of currant bread sandwiching vanilla ice cream. It is still a special treat today.

Buns and dumplings fall into the bread category, as they start with a dough made from wheat flour and yeast. However, following ancient Chinese traditions, they are often stuffed and usually steamed, although some buns are baked after steaming. Flatbreads and wrappers, used for folding around morsels of food and for spring rolls, are made from rice or wheat flour and baked on griddles, or left in the sun to dry.

In shopping malls and food courts in Singapore, there is invariably a bakery that sells many unusual types of bread – buns filled with red bean paste and almond paste; cream-filled rolls and toasted sandwiches filled with barbecued pork and pork floss. The ubiquitous restaurant item of prawns (shrimp) on sesame toast would, of course, not exist without the wide acceptance of bread.

Another culinary phenomenon is the emergence of *kaya* toast. *Kaya* is a conserve or jam, made with eggs, sugar and coconut milk and intended to top steamed glutinous rice. Along with imported British jams and butter, it became a favourite spread for toast in the Colonial era. Coffee shops that were once rustic food shops have been upgraded and smartened up to sell coffee and *kaya* toast. There are now even franchises offering this delicious breakfast fare.

Below: Eggs, sugar and coconut make a popular spread, kaya, *for toast and bread.*

Above: Indian flat breads sprinkled with sugar are a popular mid-morning snack.

Chinese chefs are also adept at making a variety of delicious steamed breads, most are made from rice flour to be eaten with braised pork dishes. These fat little buns, which are called *mun dou*, are made to fold over like a balled fist and appear on most Chinese restaurant menus.

INDIAN BREADS

To the Indian community in Singapore, when bread is mentioned it refers specifically to those from the sub-continent. The Indian workers that arrived in the early 19th century brought with them their own breads, which are quite different from the Western loaf. They came from both north and south India and introduced naans, rotis, chapatis, hoppers, puries and parathas to the region.

Although rice is grown in the Punjab and Pakistan, north Indian meals are built around breads, unlike in the south where rice holds sway. The mode of eating is with the fingers and breads make perfect edible spoons to scoop up curry and korma gravies.

The chapati is the basic unleavened Indian bread, resembling a Mexican tortilla. Flat, rough and thick, this round pancake is the staple of the community. When made thick, it is called roti. Parathas are heavier, layered and shallow-fried, eaten plain or stuffed with minced (ground) lamb. Naan is a tandoor-baked leavened bread made from white flour although most others are made with wholemeal flour (*atar*) or pounded barley, millet or buckwheat. Channa, also called besan or gram flour, made from chick peas, is also used for breads and dumplings.

From south India comes an incredible range of breakfast breads or "hoppers". Some are made with milk and others with egg and the leavening ingredient is toddy, a coconut water by-product. Thin string hoppers, which are popular in Sri Lanka, are made from Chinese rice flour, as is *puttu*, a steamed, unsweetened crumbly pastry bread with coconut. These are delicious eaten with melted palm sugar. *Iddlis* are featherlight, slightly sour crumpets made with rice flour and lentils, and *thosais* are like Scottish oatcakes.

How to make chapatis

Unlike the tandoor-baked breads, you do not need any special equipment to make chapatis, as they can be cooked in a griddle or large frying pan.

MAKES 10–12
   250g/9oz wholemeal (whole-wheat) flour
   115g/4oz plain (all-purpose) flour
   pinch of salt
   200ml/7fl oz/scant 1 cup lukewarm water

1 Sift both the flours with the salt into a large bowl and make a well in the centre. Add the water, a little at a time, and stir with a wooden spoon until the dough comes together and forms a ball that is soft and pliant but not sticky.

2 Knead the dough until all the flour is absorbed and nothing sticks to the sides of the bowl. Place the dough on a lightly floured board. With the heel of one hand, knead the dough.

3 Fold and knead again for 10 minutes. The longer you knead the lighter your chapatis will be. Reshape the ball of dough and return it to the bowl. Cover with a damp cloth and leave to rest at room temperature for half an hour.

4 Knead again once or twice and divide the dough into 10–12 even-sized pieces. Use a knife rather than tearing and stretching the dough. Roll each piece into a round ball. Flour the board if necessary to make rolling easier.

5 With a rolling pin, flatten each chapati until you get an even circle about 15cm/6in in diameter. Stack the rounds as you finish them and cover the stack with a clean damp cloth to prevent drying out.

6 Heat a large, preferably nonstick, frying pan or griddle until very hot. Cook each chapati until bubbles appear on the top side, then flip it over. This should take no more than a minute or two.

7 Cook the other side for 40 seconds and remove the pan from the heat. With a perforated spoon, lift the chapati and hold it over the naked flame for a few seconds. It should puff up nicely. Keep the bread warm while you cook the other rounds, and serve them warm and fresh with curry.

VEGETABLES

Shopping for vegetables and fruit is an everyday activity for most cooks. In rural Malaysia, makeshift stalls are set up to sell local vegetables and fruit, but most people head to the wet markets. Every day, vegetables and fruit are taken over the causeway from Johor into Singapore, as the island is totally dependent on Malaysia for its fresh agricultural produce and water. As the wet markets fill up, the stalls begin to transform into a maze of colour and bustling activity.

In general, most vegetable dishes and salads are presented as side dishes to accompany rice or a main dish and grilled (broiled) meats. Some vegetable dishes are served as meals on their own, particularly among vegetarian Indians, who produce exciting dishes that combine Indian and Malay styles. Crisp salads and raw pickled vegetables often accompany grilled meat and fish, and the Indonesian and Malay specialities, such as *rojak* and *kerabu*, are served as snacks at hawker stalls.

AUBERGINE/EGGPLANT/BRINJAL

Technically a fruit, but eaten as a vegetable, the aubergine originally came from India and Thailand. The most common variety in Singapore is long and thin, in shades of pale green and purple. The flavour is sweet, with very little bitterness. Incredibly versatile, it is added to stews, curries and stir-fries, so that the flesh absorbs all the delicious spices and flavours of the dish.

Look for smooth, unblemished skin and firm flesh. Smaller varieties range from green to purple and yellow. Much loved by Thais, they feature in dishes around South-east Asia and are usually halved and added to curries. Tiny, green pea aubergines are also popular throughout South-east Asia. The size of garden peas, these grow in clusters and have a slightly bitter taste with a pleasantly crunchy texture.

BAMBOO SHOOTS

A giant grass, indigenous to China and other tropical regions, bamboo has many important uses. The long, thin stems or "trunks" are used for making baskets, furniture and even as containers for roasting rice. They are also made into kitchen utensils, such as steamers, strainers and chopsticks. The leaves (usually dried) are used as wrappers for Chinese dumplings or steamed rice dishes, imparting their own unique flavour. The small, pine cone-sized shoots that are dug up just before they emerge from the ground have an astringent taste. Fresh, pickled or dried, bamboo shoots are popular throughout both countries, and are the key ingredient in *popiah*, the Nonya spring roll.

The fresh young shoots need only be blanched briefly. With older shoots, the outer sheaths are stripped off and the tough base removed. Once peeled, the pale yellow inner core is sliced and boiled for at least half an hour until tender.

Left: Aubergines may be long and thin or small and round.

The shoots are added to stir-fries, curries and soups. Dried shoots, mainly from China, require long soaking before use. Fresh shoots are available in Asian stores, but cans of ready-cooked shoots preserved in brine can be bought in most supermarkets.

BITTER MELON/BITTER GOURD

This gourd looks like a fat, knobbly pale green cucumber and is, in fact, a bitter relative. The bitterness comes from high levels of quinine, and it is eaten as much for its medicinal value as its flavour. Before cooking, it needs to be sliced into rounds or slit lengthways to remove the red seeds and inner membrane. The pieces can be stir-fried, blanched or pickled, or added to curries. A smaller variety from India and Sri Lanka is puréed as a health tonic by both Chinese and Indians. If you want to remove some of the bitterness, sprinkle on a little salt after slicing, leave for 10 minutes and then squeeze out the moisture.

Bitter melons are sold fresh in most Asian stores. They are best when firm and green. When they turn a little yellow, they should be cooked immediately before they turn mushy.

Above: Long beans taste similar to French or green beans.

LONG BEANS

Sometimes referred to as "snake beans", "runner beans" or "chopstick beans", these long, green beans are the immature pods of black-eyed beans (peas) and can measure up to 60cm/2ft in length. Generally long beans are cooked in curries, boiled and added to salads or stir-fried.

Above: Bamboo shoots are available fresh, but sliced, canned shoots are easier to find.

MOOLI/DAIKON

White in colour, this root vegetable looks very similar to a large carrot. A major feature in Japanese cooking, it is also known as white radish or daikon. It can be eaten raw but is most often pickled in vinegar to bring out its crisp, juicy, slightly astringent flavour. It is popular throughout South-east Asia for soups, salads and pickles, as well as stir-fries and stews. Mashed and steamed with rice flour it is called *luo bo kau* and is a street food staple in both countries. Mooli can be found in Asian markets and supermarkets.

FUZZY MELON

Also called hairy gourd, the fuzzy melon is about the size of bitter gourd with a fuzzy skin. Peeled and boiled, it is traditionally used in soups with pork ribs. It can also be sliced and stir-fried or added to spicy peppery soups. It is available in Asian markets but is rarely found in supermarkets.

Right: Bitter melon is highly regarded in South-east Asian cooking.

PULSES

Beans are used extensively in Singaporean Chinese cooking in sweet and savoury dishes.

Red beans

In Singapore these small beans, also called aduki beans, are usually soaked, boiled and mashed as a stuffing for sweet cakes. They are often used as a sweet base in the classic dessert known as *ice kacang* (shaved ice with syrup). *Ang tau thng* (red bean drink), cooked with rock sugar or sweet winter melon slices, is a favourite after-meal drink.

Mung beans

Whole dried mung beans, with husks on, are green, whereas the peeled ones are yellow and sold whole or split. Both require soaking before cooking. The mashed beans are made into a sweet paste that is the key ingredient in the Chinese New Year cake known as red turtle cake: red symbolizes prosperity and the turtle represents longevity.

Above: Yellow split mung beans.

Beansprouts

Ubiquitous throughout South-east Asia and Indo-China, beansprouts can be eaten raw but are usually added to stir-fried noodles for their crunch.

Right: Both mung and soya beansprouts are widely used in Singaporean cooking.

The most common sprouts come from mung beans and soya beans. They are similar in appearance, both with white stems, but soya bean heads are green, while those of mung beans are yellow. Soya beansprouts are sturdier and stronger in flavour, whereas mung beans are delicate and watery. Both types are nutritious, rich in vitamins and minerals.

Fresh sprouts can be stored in the refrigerator for up to 2–3 days. Packets of mung beansprouts are available in most supermarkets. Soya beansprouts can be found in Asian stores and some health stores.

Soya beans (dry)

These pale yellow beans are about twice the size of corn niblets and play a much larger role in Chinese cooking than being merely processed into soy sauce. Cantonese and Hakka chefs boil them well to make a subtly perfumed stock that is ideal for vegetarian meals.

For sweet drinks and desserts, soya beans are boiled, drained and sweetened with rock sugar. They make a drink that can be bought just about everywhere in Singapore, called *tau fa sui*, and with a coagulating agent added, the smooth liquid is turned into a super-soft jelly called *taufu fa*. This is a popular hawker treat, served with a syrup and eaten either hot or cold.

LUFFA SQUASH

Dark green with ridges running lengthways, luffa squash has sweet, spongy flesh and is usually harvested when about 30cm/1ft long. The outer skin is tough and inedible and has to be removed to reveal the soft, white flesh. Generally, it is sliced and used in stir-fries, omelettes and soups, in much the same way as you would cook a courgette (zucchini). Luffa squash is available in Asian markets. Unlike cucumber or young, tender courgettes, luffa is never eaten raw. Keep the fresh squash in the refrigerator, but do not store it for too long as within 2–3 days it will start to go limp. The luffa squash is also known as Chinese okra, silk squash and sponge gourd.

MUSHROOMS

Fresh and dried mushrooms are used in many dishes in Singaporean, Chinese and Nonya cooking, but less often in Malay cooking. Dried mushrooms, however, are favoured for stir-fries and savoury fillings because of their texture and delicate taste when reconstituted.

Chinese black mushrooms

Sometimes known as Chinese shiitake, these mushrooms have a distinctive flavour and a chewy texture. They are usually sold dried. After softening in

Below: Sliced straw mushrooms, showing their "umbrella" pattern.

Above: A luffa squash has a sweet, delicate flavour when young.

warm water for about 30 minutes, the stems are removed and the caps are added to stews, stir-fries and fillings. There is a Chinese belief that prominent fissures or cracks on the surface augur good luck and prosperity. They are sold in Asian markets and supermarkets, and are also canned.

Straw mushrooms

Also called bulb mushrooms, straw mushrooms look like glossy quail eggs. Usually sold in cans, the whole mushrooms are excellent in braised dishes for visual appeal and texture. When sliced, they reveal pretty cream stems. Very delicate in flavour and texture, they take to long cooking without turning mushy.

Tree ears

A fungus that grows on trees (hence its name), tree ears are also called cloud ears or wood ears. They are valued for their texture and nutritional qualities and are believed to cleanse the blood. Usually sold dried, they are thin and will swell up to six or eight times their volume to resemble frilly clumps of rubbery seaweed when soaked in water. Reconstitute dried tree ears by soaking for about 30 minutes, then drain and rinse well, and drain again. Remove any hard, woody stalks before cooking. On cooking, the mushrooms become quite translucent and gelatinous, but still retain a bite. Chinese cooks chop them and add them to stuffings for spring rolls and stir-fries. These mushrooms are particularly popular in Buddhist vegetarian dishes.

Oyster mushrooms

In the wild oyster mushrooms grow in clumps on rotting wood. The entire mushroom is of the same colour, which can be pearl grey, pink or yellow. They are now grown commercially and are widely available. Their delicate texture and subtle taste complement stir-fries, noodles and rice dishes. They need to be torn, not cut, and should not be overcooked: add them to the pan in the last few minutes of cooking.

Below: Pale, delicate oyster mushrooms should look and smell fresh, with no damp or discoloured areas.

Above: Tree ears are also known as cloud or wood ears.

ORIENTAL GREENS

Singapore imports most of its greens, as it has no agricultural industry to speak of.

Pak choi/bok choy

This perennial leafy cabbage is often confused with Chinese leaf. It is popular throughout South-east Asia and is grown widely in Thailand and Taiwan. In fact the Taiwan version has pale green stems while the common variety has ribbed, white stems. All are juicy and crunchy; the dark-green leaves are succulent and tasty.

The tender stems of small cabbages are rarely eaten raw but are often stir-fried with prawns (shrimp) or added to noodles. The leaves, which are mostly composed of water, need very quick cooking and shrink a lot in the process. In stir-frying, it is a good idea to cook the stems first for a few minutes before adding the leaves. These fresh greens are available in Asian stores and supermarkets.

Flowering cabbage

With its yellow flowers, long, slender stalks, and crisp leaves, the flowering cabbage, a member of the rape family, is much prized by the Chinese. When picked young and in flower, at its most tender and flavoursome, it is an excellent accompaniment to noodles while older choy sum are good on their own as stir-fries, especially when cooked with oyster sauce. Bundles are available in most Asian markets.

Green carrot

This is not an unripe "regular" carrot as such but a particular genus grown in China. It tastes much like a carrot and is used primarily as a key ingredient in the Chinese New Year raw fish offering. It can also be grated and used as a filler for spring rolls, or pickled.

Mustard greens

Also called Chinese cabbage, these resemble a head of lettuce such as cos (romaine) but are firmer and thicker. The leaves wrapping the heart have thick stalks and have a mildly bitter flavour. Blanched, they become more subtle. They make a classic Cantonese dish when gently poached with egg white and crab meat.

In Singapore, preserved mustard greens are more common than the fresh variety. The tender hearts and sometimes the leaves are preserved in brine. Quite salty, preserved mustard greens are integral to the Nonya classic Duck and Salted Vegetable Soup. Otherwise, they can be sliced and added to soups or omelettes. They are usually canned or vacuum-packed.

Chinese leaves

Known variously as Chinese leaves, Napa cabbage (mainly in the USA) or celery cabbage, this member of the brassica family has many uses and is widely used, as it is available all year round. There are three common varieties, which look fairly similar.

Chinese leaves have a delicate sweet aroma, with a mild cabbage flavour when cooked. The white stalk has a delicious crunch but becomes custard-soft when cooked. The leaves contrast perfectly with softer noodles and are great in stir-fries, stews and soups, or in salads. They absorb the flavours of meat or fish well, so blanch the leaves in boiling stock before frying them. They are also used for wrapping around minced pork and fish as a festive dish.

Chinese leaves can be stored for up to two weeks in the refrigerator without losing their resilience. If you find tiny black specks on the leaves, do not worry as they are quite normal and will not affect the flavour.

Water convolvulus

Also called water spinach, swamp cabbage or morning glory, this attractive leafy vegetable is traditionally grown in swamps or ponds. It is essential in the classic Nonya dish *kangkung belacan*.

This somewhat rare vegetable is sometimes found in Asian markets. It has hollow stems and tender, light-green, arrow-shaped leaves. When cooked, the stem tips stay firm, but the leaves rapidly become limp. It is highly perishable and must be used promptly.

Preparing water convolvulus

1 Slit the hollow stalks right down their length to check for creepy-crawlies! Separate them from the leaves and split lengthways.

2 Trim off the end bits that usually have a few rootlets. Slice into 7.5cm/3in pieces.

3 Tear off leafy stems or cut into similar lengths so each stem has a few leaves. Individual leaves, if they are small, tend to shrink too much when cooked. Wash and drain thoroughly before cooking. Store in a plastic bag for up to 2 days when refrigerated.

WINTER MELON

Large, mild-flavoured gourds, winter melons can weigh 5.4kg/12lb or more. Egg- or pear-shaped and dark green, they are harvested in the summer (but traditionally stored for winter). The white flesh tastes like marrow or courgette (zucchini) and is believed to cool fevers. It is prepared and cooked like pumpkin, and added to soups and stir-fries. Dried, sugared winter melon slices are used as a sweetener in Chinese drinks.

Winter melons and fuzzy melons are interchangeable in recipes, as they are similar in flavour. Both come in various shapes and sizes.

CASSAVA

Also known as manioc or tapioca, cassava is a large tuber that comes in varying sizes but is usually shaped like a long radish with a thick bark. It originated in South America, and is also popular in Africa and the Caribbean. African cassava can grow as large and thick as a human thigh.

In all types, the starchy root has creamy white flesh and a subtly sweet, almost buttery flavour, sometimes with delicious nuances of almond and new potato. Steamed cassava can be

Below: A large winter melon.

Above: Sweet cassava is a versatile tuber and can be cooked in many ways.

mashed with palm sugar and coconut milk for a sweet, sticky pudding, diced and tossed with desiccated (dry unsweetened shredded) coconut or eaten as a snack.

The bitter and much larger African variety of cassava contains more cyanide compounds, which are present in all cassava at some level. Hence, it must never be eaten raw as it can cause severe reactions.

Tapioca flour

This silky flour is made from the starch of the cassava root. A substitute for cornflour (cornstarch) as a thickener for sauces and custards for ice cream, it is also used to make rice papers and give them a sheen.

Tapioca pearls

Also called sago in Singapore, tapioca pearls are made from tapioca flour and come in various sizes. Sold dried, they have to be boiled until they turn translucent, then rinsed under cold water to wash off the starch. Sago is the key ingredient, with palm sugar and coconut milk, in the famous *gula Melaka* dessert.

Above: Tapioca or sago pearls prepared for drying on trays.

JICAMA

This root vegetable looks like a large turnip or swede and has an apple-like crunch and delicate sweet taste rather similar to water chestnut. Peel and cut into chunks or slices for soups, salads and stir-fries. It is a key ingredient in the Malaysian spicy salad called *rojak*.

LOTUS ROOT AND SEEDS

Held with great reverence since ancient times, the lotus plant is rife with symbolism. It is a beautiful aquatic plant with delicate pink and white flowers, closely associated with the Chinese deity Guanyin, the goddess of mercy and patron saint of sailors, who is always pictured carrying a lotus stem.

The plant is edible in its entirety. The stamens are infused to make a fragrant tisane; the seeds are dried and boiled for sweets and cakes; the leaves are used for wrapping rice and steamed snacks; the stems are added to salads, soups and braised dishes. Lotus roots are juicy and fragrant, and when sliced reveal a lacy pattern of holes.

In ancient Chinese tradition, the nourishing lotus root is believed to aid blood circulation and to improve virility. In Singapore, the lotus root is added to

Above: The flesh of a jicama is a cross between an apple and a potato.

Preparing cassava

1 Scrub the root and either peel with a vegetable peeler or run a sharp knife into the skin around the girth at 7.5cm/3in intervals. Then cut down and each piece of skin will come away easily.

2 Cut the white flesh into chunks, removing the fibrous core.

3 Drop the pieces into a bowl of acidulated water to prevent discoloration. Drain, then boil, steam, bake or fry the cassava pieces until tender.

Right: Taro is a rough-skinned tuber used both as a fruit and a vegetable.

soups with pork ribs, or stir-fried. The roots, stems and seeds of the lotus plant are available fresh, dried and preserved, in most Asian stores. If dried, all of them need to be soaked overnight before being cooked.

TARO

This root, known as taro or yam, comes in varying sizes from little egg-shaped nuggets to barrel shapes the size of grapefruit. All have a fuzzy brown skin with white or purple-flecked flesh.

The Chinese cook taro with duck and chicken. They also steam and mash it to wrap minced (ground) meat for dim sum dumplings. The Teochews make a dessert called *orh nee* from mashed and braised taro paste with a lot of sugar. Nonya cooking also features the tender stalks of young taro in curries. Long and thick, it is peeled and cut into short pieces before being cooked. Its spongy texture absorbs the flavour and sauce of a dish.

Taro tends to be used as a fruit, to be sliced, battered and deep-fried as a snack or diced and cooked with sweet potato in a popular dessert called *bubur cha cha*. All types have a similar distinctive nutty flavour and crumbly texture when cooked. Taro roots are available in Asian stores as well as in some supermarkets.

Below: Fresh lotus roots, which are in fact rhizomes, look like linked sausages. The papery leaves and light-coloured seeds are also widely used.

WATER CHESTNUT

Water chestnuts are grown in flooded paddy fields but harvested when the soil is dry. When they are sold fresh in the markets, they are often covered with crumbly earth. Each is about the size of a large chestnut and, once peeled, reveals a chalk white, sweet meat. Juicy and crunchy at the same time, the texture is reminiscent of an Asian pear.

Regarded as cooling and beneficial to the digestive system, water chestnuts are also believed to sweeten the breath. They are high in starch and nutrients, including copper. They can be eaten raw in salads, or chopped up and added to fillings for spring rolls or stir-fries. They can also be ground into flour to make water chestnut dim sum.

Fresh water chestnuts have a short life span and must be eaten within 2–3 days of purchase. Cans of peeled and ready-cooked water chestnuts are available in most supermarkets. Once opened, store water chestnuts in water in the refrigerator for up to a week, changing the water daily.

FRUIT

Traditionally, fruit is eaten at the end of a meal to cleanse the palate or aid the digestion, while sweet puddings and cakes are nibbled as snacks. Many of the tropical fruits eaten in Singapore are now available in Asian markets and large supermarkets.

BANANAS

For most Singaporeans, bananas are eaten not merely as a fruit but turn up in many cooked dishes. The most popular type is called *pisang rajah* ("king of bananas"), which has an exquisite perfume. They are sold as fried bananas or made into banana fritters. Other varieties range from finger-length perfumed bananas to the enormous elephant tusk banana, which can be 30cm/12in long. This is sliced and cooked with coconut milk and sugar in a dessert called *penghat*.

The banana plant may look like a palm tree but is in reality a perennial herb. It grows a new "trunk" every year and after blossoming and fruiting, dies back to its roots. Each tree may have up to half a dozen bunches, each bunch containing many "hands" with anything up to a dozen fruits on each hand.

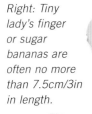

Right: Tiny lady's finger or sugar bananas are often no more than 7.5cm/3in in length.

Right: When very ripe, small apple bananas have a faint taste and aroma of fresh apple.

Above: Banana leaves are not eaten but are often used to wrap food.

Banana leaves

Held in high regard as a natural wrapper, this "green foil" does multiple duty as plates, table mats or shaped into intriguing containers for steaming, baking and grilling (broiling), especially in traditional Indonesian and Malaysian cooking. The leaves are blanched in very hot water to make them pliable and wiped dry before use. Fresh banana leaves are available in Asian and African supermarkets. They do not freeze well as they tend to crack when thawed.

Banana blossom/bud

Each large, deep purple bud of the banana tree contains pale yellow, finger-sized blossoms in thick clusters. They are edible and are enjoyed throughout South-east Asia as a delicate vegetable, especially in Nonya cooking where they take pride of place as a Chinese New Year salad. The purple husks are inedible but make beautiful "plates" for salads and other dishes. The blossoms are

Above: At the heart of the banana flower lies the delicate banana bud.

sliced, blanched and tossed with coconut cream, cooked prawns (shrimp) and chilli and shrimp paste sambal. They can also be eaten raw but are slightly bitter. Soak them in water with lemon or lime juice to prevent them discolouring.

COCONUT

The coconut tree is revered as the "tree of life" and is imported from Malaysia. Practically every part is used: the leaves make great wrappers for compressed rice cakes boiled and served as the classic accompaniment to satay; the spines of the leaves are trimmed and made into skewers; the trunks are used as piles in building; and the nut has a myriad of uses. The flesh of young nuts is eaten as a sweetmeat and that of older nuts is grated and squeezed for milk, which plays a vital role, like cow's milk in the West.

The outer hard shell is shaped, turned and fashioned into ladles and cups. What we buy is only the stone of the actual fruit; the husk and fibres are removed in the country of origin and used as stuffing for mattresses, as fuel, or woven into ropes. Excess coconut meat is usually smoked into copra for export and for making coconut oil.

When you shake a coconut you should hear the swishing sound of the water inside. Pierce the eyes on top of

Below: Creamed coconut block.

the coconut and pour out the water. To open a coconut, place it on a flat surface and use a cleaver or hammer to tap it hard all the way round. Pull the shell apart and pry the flesh out with a knife or sharp-edged spoon. Slice the thin brown skin off the flesh and chop or grate the pieces for further use. To facilitate extracting the meat, place the coconut in a fairly hot oven for about 15 minutes until it cracks. The flesh comes away more easily this way.

Coconut milk

This is the cream of Singapore and fundamental in most curries and puddings. Its savoury sweetness lends a unique flavour to every dish that is cooked with it, the rich quality blending beautifully with spices, sugar and other aromatics. Its creaminess is much loved by Malays and Nonyas and it is thickened with cornflour (cornstarch) to make a blancmange-like custard. The common practice is to squeeze grated coconut for its "first milk" with a scant amount of water. More water is added to yield a "second milk" to be used in a variety of dishes. Once you have squeezed out all the coconut milk, allow it to settle in the bowl and the cream will rise to the top. This can be skimmed off, if you wish to use it separately.

Coconut milk does not keep well and is usually made daily. It can turn rancid very quickly and is best refrigerated if you are not using it immediately. It is widely available in cans and cartons.

Coconut oil

Coconut cream, when simmered for a long time until the milk solids evaporate, renders down to a rich, aromatic oil. This is used mainly for frying spices to make rich curries. It is a saturated fat that turns solid very quickly.

Green coconut water

The coconut water used for cooking is extracted from young, green coconuts. Each nut yields about 300ml/½ pint of liquid. The slightly astringent water is drunk neat as a cooling thirst quencher. All over rural Asia stalls sell young coconut water, which is the most natural of drinks with no additives. It makes an effective rising agent in many Nonya and Malay rice flour cakes, and is used as a tenderizing agent for tough meat. Mild and sweet, it features in a number of braised dishes and Malay cakes. It is even used as a shampoo by Indians. Although you can use the water from ripened nuts, it is best to look in Asian markets for a young coconut.

Above: Coconut is versatile and a valuable crop.

Making coconut milk

While most wet markets sell ready-grated coconut for making milk, or tins of prepared milk, it is easy to make yourself.

1 Grate the flesh from a fresh coconut, or shred it in a food processor.

2 Put the grated flesh into a bowl and knead thoroughly. Squeeze out the creamy "first milk".

3 Pour roughly 600ml/1 pint/ 2½ cups warm water over the shreds. Stir and leave to steep for 30 minutes. Line a sieve (strainer) with muslin (cheesecloth) over a bowl and ladle the coconut into it.

4 Gather the muslin in your hands and squeeze out any excess liquid. This is the "second milk."

Above: The leaves and rind of kaffir limes impart a distinctive, zesty flavour.

CUSTARD APPLE

Originating from tropical America, the custard apple was introduced to Singapore by the Portuguese. The fruits are heart-shaped, buff or green and about 10cm/4in in diameter. The skin is thick and may have small bumps depending on the variety. The flesh is creamy white and granular, surrounding a fibrous central core. Small black seeds are embedded in the flesh, which has a custard-like consistency and is slightly astringent but sweet when ripe.

DURIAN

This large fruit encased in deep-green armour-like skin with fearsome-looking spikes has had much bad press, often unjustified. Most airlines and hotels ban the fruit but many Singaporeans love it. If you can put up with the strong, indescribable odour, the buttery yellow flesh is delicious, with nut and honey overtones, quite unlike any other fruit.

Durians are much sought after and used to be seasonal but are now available all year round. They are expensive and are only available in some Asian markets. The best ones come from Malaysia and have a slightly bitter edge. Thai durians tend to be woody and dry. Avoid any fruits that have split.

To prepare durian, a wooden blade is forced into the natural seams across the length of the fruit. Inside are four or five indented shells containing large pieces of fleshy pulp. There is no way to eat durian other than with the hands. The flesh is tugged or sucked and licked from the large seeds.

GUAVA

A native of Brazil, the guava was taken by the Portuguese in the 17th century to the Philippines and gradually spread across South-east Asia. Grown widely in Malaysia, the different types vary in shape and size. The thick skin ranges from white to pale green, pink or red, and the flesh may be white, yellow or pink and contain many small hard pips. Guavas have a characteristic aroma ranging from rose blossom to mango. They are eaten mainly as a dessert fruit, but are also sliced and mixed with a sambal for a relish that complements many dishes.

JACKFRUIT

Large and spiky, the jackfruit looks similar to a durian but with short stubs instead of spikes. It can grow as large as two rugby balls. There are two distinct types: *nangka* and *chempedak*. When sliced open, nangka reveals a cluster of yellow fruit, each encircling a large seed. The texture is delightfully crunchy and tastes like ripe mangoes.

Above: A durian and its large seeds.

Chempedak is more fragrant, with nuances of pineapple and apricot, and the flesh is creamy and chewy at the same time. Packed with vitamins, the fruit is enjoyed on its own as well as mixed in a tropical fruit salad. The seeds can be boiled or roasted as a snack. Unripe jackfruit is also cooked in coconut milk curries.

LIME

In Singapore, fresh green limes are generally used for their juice but they are also pickled or dried as sweetmeats. The juice has a sharp tang that enhances the flavour of other ingredients. The rind is grated and added to savoury dishes. The leaves of

Below: Jackfruit are very large, and a single fruit can weigh up to 40kg/88lb.

Above: Red-skinned mangoes are eaten as a fruit or in desserts, and green-skinned ones as a vegetable.

kaffir limes are unique in their heady, zesty fragrance and prized in Nonya sambals and curries, shredded and added at the last minute. They are available, dried, in many Asian stores and markets.

Below: Papayas, often known as paw paw, are one of the most attractive tropical fruits.

LYCHEE

Native to the sub-temperate regions of China and north Thailand, lychees have thin, mauve-pink, bumpy skins that are easily peeled to reveal very juicy, white flesh covering a black seed. A superior variety from China, when in season, boasts of very thick flesh encasing one or no seed. Lychees are also available canned in syrup.

LONGAN

These fruits are found in most sub-tropical regions in South-east Asia and have smooth, brown skins with vague black spots. The crisp skin is easily removed and the flesh is firm, crunchy and sweet, covering small black seeds. Longans keep well in the refrigerator and are delicious chilled. They are seasonal, but can be found all year round sold in cans, in their own juice or in a light syrup.

MANGO

Originally from India, several varieties of mango are also grown in Malaysia and Singapore. The sweetest come from Thailand: thick, round and tapered at one end, they are called elephant tusk mangoes. Mango skins may be yellow, pale orange or green and ripened ones are eaten mainly as a fruit. The sweet yellow or orange flesh is wonderfully

Above: Mangosteens have a fragrant, delicate flavour and are best eaten raw.

thirst-quenching, with a lovely aroma of pine, and is also a good source of vitamin A. There are also green mangoes that never change colour – these are sliced or shredded and used mainly in salads.

MANGOSTEEN

These handsome fruits are apple-sized with a smooth, thick purple rind. This is partially covered by the flower petals, which remain attached as the fruit ripens. Inside, the pulp is chalk white and divided into five to seven segments. The large segments contain a seed, while the smaller segments are seedless. The flesh is astringent with a delicious perfume. Singaporeans eat them as a cooling treat, especially after a surfeit of durians, as mangosteens ripen just after the spiky fruit.

PAPAYA

Indigenous to South America and tropical Asia, the gourd-like fruit comes in varying sizes, from about 250g/8oz to giants of 1.3kg/3lb or more. The flesh is orange or pale yellow and can have a delicious perfume. Papayas are full of vitamins and honey-sweet.

A favourite Malaysian and Thai salad called *som tam* uses a variety that remains green and never ripens. Peeled and finely sliced or shredded, it is tossed with ground dried shrimp, lime juice, fish sauce, chillies and garlic.

Below: Pineapples make a delicious after dinner snack.

PINEAPPLE

Grown throughout South-east Asia, pineapples vary in size, juiciness and sweetness. They do double duty as a dessert fruit, when ripe, and as a sweet addition to Singapore salads and Nonya seafood curries. Look for pineapples with firm skin, with a good orange colouring and a fragrant odour. To prepare fresh pineapple slices, first slice off the leaves, then use a sharp knife to cut off the skin in vertical strips. Make diagonal cuts all along the fruit, removing all the black eyes, then slice the whole fruit lengthways into four quarters and remove the hard, pithy core. Finally cube or slice into rings.

RAMBUTAN

Shaggy-haired and alien-looking, rambutans resemble hairy plums. There are a number of varieties, varying in sweetness and coloured with streaks of gold, orange and green. The market variety tends to be red.

Right: Rambutans have a distinctive skin covered in soft spiky hairs. They are available fresh and ready prepared in cans.

Above right: Bright yellow star fruit is used in snacks, drinks and savoury dishes.

Easy to open, the hairy shells encase a translucent white fruit with a pale stone (pit) in the middle. The flesh is crunchy, cool and sweet.

SAPODILLA

The size of kiwi fruit, these originate from Central America but are widely grown in Malaysia, Thailand and India, where they are variously known as *chiko* or *chiku*. They have a light, slightly fuzzy skin that when peeled reveals a soft, tan flesh with black pips. The texture is luscious, like a soft pear, and tastes of burnt sugar. They are available mainly at Indian greengrocers and in some South-east Asian markets.

SOUR STAR FRUIT

Related to star fruit, sour star fruit is found widely in South-east Asia and other high altitude tropical regions, where it is variously called camia, cucumber tree and tree sorrel. The fruits resemble green or pale yellow miniature cucumbers, up to 10cm/4in long and the thickness of a thumb. They grow in clusters on the tree trunk. The skin is very thin and smooth, and the fruits have very few small seeds.

A favourite ingredient in Malay and Nonya sambals, relishes and pickles, they are very tart with a crunchy texture. They are not widely available but may be found in some South-east Asian markets.

SOURSOP

Often mistaken for a durian, soursop grows widely in humid tropical countries, especially in the coastal regions of Malaysia. The fruit, often kidney shaped, may weigh as much as 3kg/8lb, and is borne on thick, woody stalks. The thick skin is dark green with rows of soft green stubby spikes. The pulp is very soft, white and creamy and very juicy, ranging from tart to sweet flavours. Buried within the flesh are many shiny, black seeds. A rich source of vitamin C, they are often puréed for their juice. They are available in South-east Asian and Chinese markets.

STAR FRUIT

Also known as carambola in South America, this star-shaped fruit has five wedges and is sweet with a slightly astringent taste. In Singapore, the ripened yellow fruit is enjoyed as a juicy snack or pulped for its refreshing juice. The green immature fruit is finely sliced and served as a tangy vegetable, salted and dried as a pickle ingredient, or tossed in salads. Available in some Asian markets, they have a short shelf life: avoid any fruits that have dark spots.

TOFU PRODUCTS

Far from being regarded as a "poor man's meat", tofu or soy bean curd is revered among Chinese communities throughout Asia. Protein-rich and low in calories, tofu is devoid of cholesterol, which is found only in products of animal origin. It also provides essential amino acids, vitamins and minerals. It is made by combining soya bean milk with a coagulant such as gypsum powder to form curds, which are then compressed into blocks of varying densities. While it has a neutral flavour – some call it tasteless – tofu's very blandness is great for absorbing other flavours. It is firm enough to be added to stir-fries and used as a container for various stuffings, and adds healthy bulk to soups, braised vegetarian dishes and spring roll fillings.

FRESH TOFU

These soft white blocks packed in water are available in most Asian markets. The UHT varieties are also available in most supermarkets. Generally, soft tofu is better for soups and steamed dishes, whereas the firm variety is best in stir-fries and fillings. Tofu is best used straight away, but if it is submerged in water, changed daily, it can be stored, chilled, for 3–4 days.

DRIED TOFU

Also known as "bean curd sticks" in Singapore, this product is made by simmering soya milk until a thin skin forms on top, which shrinks and stiffens when dried. Creamy white in colour with a subtle flavour, tofu sticks are sold in Asian markets. They must be soaked in water to soften for about 30 minutes before use.

FRIED TOFU

Firm tofu, deep-fried until it forms a brown skin, is used for the popular Malay street food dish *tauhu goreng*, dressed with shredded cucumber, boiled beansprouts and a spicy peanut sauce. A Chinese variety, called *tau kwa pok*, is tofu that has been rendered completely dry. The light, spongy brown cakes are split open and stuffed with braised duck, chicken or vegetables, with spicy chilli and vinegar sauce.

PRESERVED TOFU

Cubes of fresh tofu that have been preserved in brine for several months have a strong flavour and need to be rinsed before use. They can be used sparingly to add extra flavour to stir fries and other vegetable and meat dishes. Preserved tofu is sold in Asian stores.

Above, clockwise from top: Pressed, silken and firm tofu, all varying in degrees of firmness and suited to stir-fries or soups.

Above: Cubes of fermented tofu.

FERMENTED TOFU

Fresh tofu is fermented on beds of rice straw, then dried in the sun before marinating with salt, Chinese grain wine and spices. It is stored in brine in sealed earthenware crocks and left to mature for at least six months. It is a favourite condiment with rice congee and is used in marinating poultry and as a rich seasoning for braised dishes.

TOFU SKINS

These are made by lifting the skin of tofu as it is made and then dried flat as brown, wrinkly sheets. With storage they become brittle and crack easily when handled. If so, they have to be moistened slightly with a damp towel before being used as spring roll wrappers. A classic Nonya spring roll called *bak kng* uses these skins.

TOFU WAFERS

These are light, brown pieces of slightly sweetened, dried tofu pieces that can be fried as crackling to top stir-fried noodles or added to vegetable stews. The Chinese call them *dim choke*.

SILKEN TOFU AND TOFU MILK

Soft, silken tofu, or *tau hu fa*, is a popular dessert in Singapore, where it is served in a very sweet syrup perfumed with pandan leaves. There are vendors in food courts and hawker centres throughout Singapore selling this cold or warm snack. The tofu is freshly made and entirely different from UHT silken tofu. The same stalls also sell *tou fa shui* – tofu milk or soy bean milk – a hugely popular and cooling milk drink.

FISH AND SHELLFISH

The coastal waters off Singapore are home to a rich variety of tropical fish and shellfish. Neighbouring Malaysia is blessed with a large network of river systems, starting in the mountain ranges and flowing through the rainforests to the sea. Every town and village has a wet market where fishmongers sell absolutely fresh fish that were swimming in their ocean or river habitat just hours earlier. Coastal communities eat more fish than meat, and fish cooking is taken to great heights.

Fish preparation varies between the races and communities. Indians use a lot of tuna, manifest in the famous fish head curry. Malay and Nonya cooks grind fish into paste, add spices and wrap them in banana leaves for grilling (broiling) or steaming to make a dish called *otak otak*. Malays also deep-fry anchovies until crisp and serve them with coconut rice. Chinese cooks fry large fish whole and bathe them in lots of sweet and sour sauce or black bean sauce.

In the past decade, there has been a trend started among hawker stalls to serve grilled ray fish with *sambal belacan* (spicy chilli and shrimp paste sambal). Singapore chilli crab has also gained a global reputation as an iconic dish, and dozens of stalls and restaurants along the East Coast offer it. Another national dish in Singapore is oyster omelette (*or luak*), in which plump oysters are fried with egg. Some stalls also use barnacles for this dish but both versions are equally delicious.

Fish balls are staple hawker fare, they can be eaten simply as they are served in a hot stock, or they can be eaten with all kinds of noodles. Prawns (shrimp) and squid are also processed into small balls, each the size of a cherry tomato. Whatever seafood is cooked, it must be absolutely fresh and locals will not buy or cook the frozen variety if they can help it. Until the 1950s, refrigeration was rare in Singapore, and all fish bought had to be cooked on the same day. This has honed the local taste buds to expect nothing but the freshest.

ANCHOVY, LONG-JAWED ANCHOVY

One of Singapore's best-loved fish and a well-documented export, anchovies or *ikan bilis* are best known in their dried form, bilis. They form the staple seafood in coconut rice or *nasi lemak*. Fresh bilis are relatively rare these days except in coastal rural Malaysian towns. Steamed whole or deboned and deep-fried, they make delicious crunchy eating.

EELS

Adult eels have almost black backs and silvery bodies. Females tend to be much heavier than males – often three times as heavy – and are highly prized in stewed Chinese dishes with wine and ginger. They are almost always sold live as they deteriorate quickly, especially in the tropics. They are hard to prepare but if you rub the skin with plenty of salt you can grip it firmly. Or you can ask the fishmonger to skin them for you and to chop them into 5cm/2in lengths.

HARDTAIL/TORPEDO TREVALLY

The name of this fish comes from a peculiar hard ridge from the tail to halfway up the body. It can measure up to 50cm/20in and is bluish-green above and silvery below, with dusky grey fins.

Above: Buy firm fish, such as glossy mackerel, for spicy and fragrant sauces.

Easily recognized because of its torpedo-like body, numerous finlets and stiff thin tail, it is best grilled or steamed. The hard ridge must be sliced off before cooking, so you can remove the meat from the tail end easily.

HERRING

While the common name is herring, these fish are also called sprat or rainbow sardine. Growing to about 15cm/6in with a dark green back and silver belly, they have very fine bones. They are very tasty when fried and eaten with a chilli dip. Larger fish can be gutted and filleted before cooking.

MACKEREL

The mackerel family embraces several species but the most common is known as Spanish mackerel, with dark grey backs, silvery sides and roughly circular spots. They range from 17.5cm/7in long to large fish of up to 43cm/17in. They are a nutritious fish with a rich flavour. Excellent to eat when very fresh, mackerel has delicate, sweet flesh and is most often fried or cooked in sour fish curries.

Preparing fish

With very few exceptions, this is how any fresh, whole fish should be prepared. The head is generally left on: most Chinese prefer not to behead fish in the belief that no living creature should go to the next life decapitated.

1 Wear rubber gloves to protect your hands from the smell of fish if you wish. Holding the fish firmly, make a slit down the belly and remove all entrails.

2 Where the gills join the body at each corner, snip to separate them and remove the gills. With a sharp pair of scissors trim away all fins, cutting close to the body. Wash and pat dry. Coat with a little cornflour (cornstarch) if deep or shallow frying whole, as this gives a crisp coating.

3 To fillet the trimmed fish, lay it on the chopping board and hold it firmly with the tail end towards you. Cut away from you with a sharp knife flat against the central bone. Turn the fish over to cut off the second fillet. Keep or freeze all trimmings as they make excellent fish stock.

POMFRET/PORGY

These distinctively shaped fish have no pelvic fins and come in two main species, black or white. Both types range in size from 12.5cm/5in to as large as 23cm/9in. White pomfrets (porgy) have a delicate flesh much loved by Teochews, and are usually simply steamed with a little ginger. Black pomfret have a robust flavour and firmer flesh and are usually fried or grilled to be eaten with *sambal belacan*.

RED SNAPPER

One of the most important groups of local fish in Singapore, snappers are highly esteemed and easily recognized by their straight ventral profile with pointed snout. These snap when they are caught, hence their name. Most are brightly coloured, ranging from deep red in the larger species to shocking pink, silver and yellow, usually with lines and spots. They have a delicate flavour and are usually cooked in curries or fried whole.

SEA BASS

A fine fish, sea bass have variable but always striking coloration, from silvery to light brown to orange with large-edged blue spots. They have a sleek shape rather like a salmon, and can grow to a length of 90cm/36in and weigh up to 7kg/15½lb. The white flesh is firm and delicately flavoured and tastes best when simply steamed. It can be marinated with spices and wrapped in a banana leaf before cooking.

SNAKEHEAD

This eel-like fish is highly prized for its meaty flesh and full flavour, and features in Cantonese fish and rice vermicelli soup (*yue tau mifun*). The fish are usually sold live. They have a near-black, slippery skin and are often mistaken for fat eels. They can turn up in many guises, in curries, grilled, fried or flaked for relishes.

STINGRAY

Although the normal variety is relatively small, about 30cm/12in across its widest part, stingrays can also grow to enormous size, weighing as much as 200kg/450lb. They may be coloured from sandy to dark brown or marked with numerous spots, but a better recognition point is their whip-like tail. Grilled or fried, they have a similar flavour and texture to skate.

THREADFIN/TASSEL FISH

Probably the most expensive fish of all and quite rare, these fish are almost boneless with a delicate sweet flesh reminiscent of cod or halibut. They are large, up to 120cm/4ft long, and are mostly sold as steaks or cutlets. They are silvery-green above with a creamy belly and the name refers to the four threads on each pectoral fin. Some species have black dorsal tips to their fins and green tassels.

TREVALLY

Not to be confused with torpedo trevally (see facing page), these popular fish range from large yellow-bellied ones to silvery grey small ones, and have a characteristic yellow tail fin. A very meaty fish highly esteemed in Malaysia and Thailand, trevally is also known as kingfish in Africa. It is best simply fried or cooked in a curry.

Below: Sea bass is fleshy and versatile, ideal for stews and curries.

TUNA

While tuna can grow to a very large size, the most common and popular ones in Singapore are the smaller bluefin tuna, about 50cm/20in long. Characterized by a blue-black top and silvery belly, tuna have to keep swimming continuously in order to maintain a supply of oxygen. This results in strong muscle, the part of the fish that makes the best eating. The flesh is generally pale but can vary from pink to deep red, and is usually sold as steaks because of the fish's large size. The head is highly prized for Indian fish head curry but it also tastes good fried or grilled (broiled).

WOLF HERRING/DORAB

Specimens up to 60cm/24in long have been caught in deep waters off Asian coasts but the market variety is usually around 45cm/18in long. The fish has a bluish-green back with silvery sides that go grey when it has been dead a while.

Preparing fresh prawns

Raw freshwater and saltwater prawns and large shrimp are either peeled before cooking or have their shells left on for certain dishes. If large, peeled raw prawns must have their intestinal tracts removed. It is not necessary to devein small shrimp.

Below: Raw prawns.

The large upturned mouth looks fearsome but the flesh has a delicate, sweet flavour, and the numerous bones cannot spoil the excellent taste and flaky texture. One of the best-loved fish in Singapore, wolf herring is the main ingredient in fish balls and a star item in the Chinese New Year raw fish treat.

ABALONE

Rarely available fresh, abalone is an expensive shellfish that comes mainly from South America and Australia and is usually sold canned. Much prized as a special festive dish during Chinese New Year, dried abalone have to be boiled for at least an hour before continuing to the next step of cooking. Many upmarket Chinese restaurants in Singapore specialize in abalone, either braised in a rich broth or sliced and cooked in Mongolian hotpots or Chinese steamboats.

CRAB

There are several varieties, the most common being mottled or flower crabs, named on account of the pale blue mottling on their shells. They are about the size of an adult palm, smaller than the large grey mud crabs. They make good eating, especially in the well-loved Singapore dish of chilli crab.

Preparing crab

Usually sold live, crabs tend to become comatose when chilled for a few hours. Make sure the crab is dry, with no sign of water sloshing around in the shell, which should be firm and contain no cracks or holes. Turn the crab belly up and remove the soft V-shaped flap on the belly. Pull the top shell off, scoop out the soft, yellowish coral and reserve. Discard the feathery gills and snap off the legs and claws. The larger claws should be cracked but not entirely broken, so the flesh can be easily extracted

Above: Preparing blue mottled crab.

when cooked. Rinse the body and cut it into two or more pieces. Alternatively, steam the crabs whole until they turn deep pink throughout.

PRAWNS (SHRIMP)

Both marine and freshwater prawns are highly prized among the Chinese in Singapore for one reason. Their Cantonese name, *ha*, reflects laughter and happiness and they are eaten for symbolic reasons during Chinese New Year. The marine variety is plentiful and comes in various sizes. Prawns have a sweet flavour and turn pink or orange when they are cooked. Buy fresh raw prawns if possible, choosing specimens that are a translucent grey colour tinged with blue. Juicy and meaty, the bigger prawns are often grilled whole, or added to stir-fries or curries; the small ones are dried and added to stocks to enhance the flavour. The small freshwater ones are more delicate and are often steamed briefly, or cooked live in the famous dish called drunken prawns.

SAND LOBSTER

The sand lobster looks like an immature lobster, and has a broad head and tiny claws. Most of the meat is contained within the body section and has much the same delicate, luxurious flavour as normal lobster. When sand lobsters are plentiful, Nonya cooks often use them in place of prawns for spiced or steamed seafood dishes.

SQUID

An important and plentiful food source, squid are consumed widely in Southeast Asia. Along with octopus and cuttlefish, they are members of the cephalopod family. Torpedo-shaped and flanked by two fins, eight short and two long tentacles, the entire body is edible and delicious. Squid is easy to prepare and can be cooked in a variety of ways, such as stir-fried with spices.

If stir-frying, slit the prepared sac from top to bottom and turn it inside out. Flatten it on a board and score the inside surface lightly with a knife, pressing just hard enough to make a crisscross pattern. Cut lengthways into ribbons, which will curl when cooked briefly.

MOLLUSCS

Like other types of shellfish, molluscs are always sold alive but deteriorate rapidly, so always cook them as soon as possible after buying. When you are shopping for bivalves such as mussels, clams and oysters, check that they contain plenty of sea water and feel heavy for their size. Do not buy any that have broken or gaping shells. When you give them a sharp tap, they should snap shut immediately. If they don't, they should be discarded. There will usually be several in each batch that you need to discard, so buy plenty.

Molluscs must be eaten within one day of purchase, but will keep perfectly well for a few hours when stored in the refrigerator. Put them in a large bowl, cover with a damp cloth and keep them

Above: Covering molluscs with a damp cloth will help keep them fresh in the coldest part of the refrigerator.

in the coldest part of the refrigerator (at 2°C/36°F) until you are ready to prepare and eat them.

Oysters can be kept for a couple of days, thanks to the sea water contained in their shells. Store them cupped side down. Never store shellfish in fresh water, or they will die. Ready-frozen bivalves should not be kept in the freezer for more than 2 months.

Preparing molluscs

Scrub bivalves under cold running water, using a stiff brush or scourer to remove any dirt or sand. Open them over a bowl to catch the delicious juice. This will be gritty, so must be strained before being used in a sauce or stock. Cockles usually contain a lot of sand but they will expel this if left overnight in a bucket of sea water or salted water.

Blood cockles

These small bivalves are very popular at seafood stalls and are usually eaten blanched until just cooked and dipped into chilli and garlic sauce. They are also often added to *char kway teow* and *laksa*. They may contain some mud and should be thoroughly rinsed.

Horn shell

Looking like little nautiluses, horn shells are boiled and eaten as a snack with chilli sauce. Peranakans cook them in a rich coconut milk curry. When they are long, you may need to snip away about 1cm/½in of the tapered end to make it easier to get at the meat with a small skewer, or just suck hard to get it out.

Mussels

These are either green lipped or brown with a pale yellow flesh. They are simply steamed or cooked in Chinese wine with garlic and ginger. When buying mussels, allow 450g/1lb per person, as the shells make up much of the weight.

Oysters

Mainly imported from Australia or New Zealand, oysters are more of a Western treat in upmarket seafood places. Those used in omelettes are a smaller variety, or barnacles are sometimes substituted.

Scallops

Served steamed with ginger and garlic, scallops make an elegant starter. As an exception to the rule about buying fresh molluscs, scallops are often sold already opened and cleaned.

Preparing squid

1 Check the squid is fresh and intact. Rinse it well in fresh water.

2 Grip the head in one hand, the body in the other, and tug the head out of the body sac, pulling most of the innards with it. Grip the top of the backbone and pull it out. Rinse the inside of the sac and pat dry.

3 Sever the arms and tentacles from the head and innards and put beside the sac. Discard the rest, including the skin.

DRIED AND FERMENTED FISH

Regarded as natural stock cubes in the kitchens of Singapore, dried and salted or fermented fish products are also frequently served in their own right as side dishes, or even as main dishes with other ingredients. Fried small dried fish and crustaceans, chillied or spiced, are enjoyed as crunchy snacks. Purist cooks still turn their noses up at store-bought stock cubes or seasoning powders and prefer to boil handfuls of dried shrimps, *ikan bilis* (sprats or anchovies), cuttlefish and dried scallops to make the requisite stock for noodles and other dishes.

DRIED SHRIMP

Originating in south India and Sri Lanka, these strongly flavoured shellfish are used in many ways. With a rich, briny flavour and a chewy texture, they have to be soaked or boiled briefly to release their distinctive taste. An important seasoning in many spice blends, especially those meant for seafood curries and *laksas*, dried shrimp are also added to sambals and condiments, usually ground with a pestle and mortar first. They come in many sizes, some so tiny as to look like little commas, others as much as 2.5cm/1in long. Coloured matt pink or light tan, dried shrimp are available in all Asian markets. They can be kept for months in an airtight jar.

Preparing dried shrimp

They should be soaked in warm water for 20 minutes for use in stock or briefly blanched in boiling water if needed as a salad dressing ingredient. This plumps them up and releases their flavour.

Grind them in a pestle and mortar until coarse or fine as required and toss with lime juice and chilli paste for a pungent dip or to flavour fried rice. Deep-fry them and mix with sliced dried chillies to use as a crunchy condiment and topping.

DRIED SQUID

These are widely available in Singapore, and are used as a crunchy ingredient in salads, or soaked until soft for Chinese dishes. Grilled (broiled) or roasted,

dried squid (*sotong*) lend pungent sweetness to soups. When soaked in water with borax powder, they turn gelatinous and pale pink. They can be sliced and added to stir-fries or soups. They are available from most Chinese markets.

DRIED ANCHOVIES

Commonly found in all Chinese shops, dried anchovies or *ikan bilis* are integral to Singaporean cooking. Sold either whole or filleted, these small, finger-length fish are used to make stock for seafood dishes, or fried until crispy to be served as a crunchy side dish with peanuts and coconut rice. When tossed in a rich chilli sambal, they also make a delicious condiment.

SALT FISH

In most coastal regions of South-east Asia any excess catch is dried and salted. Various species are preserved in this way, but the most popular and expensive salt fish are made from threadfin. Sold either as fillets or on the bone, they are generally fried to be eaten with congee by the Chinese, or cooked in curries for their rich salty flavour. They are available from all Chinese supermarkets.

SHRIMP PASTE

A traditional condiment, shrimp paste is essential to Malay and Peranakan cooks in Singapore. Toasted and ground with chillies to make *sambal belacan* it is central to almost every meal. The best shrimp paste is believed to come from Melaka. It comes in blocks or jars and should be kept refrigerated or in an airtight container.

PRAWN PASTE

Entirely different from shrimp paste, this black, tar-like ingredient (petis-Malay) is made from dried extract of prawns and used mainly as a salad dressing in tandem with chilli paste and lime juice. Extremely thick, it is easier to work with when liquefied with a little warm water. Available in most Chinese stores, it should be kept in an air-tight tin after opening because of the strong smell.

Preparing shrimp paste

Shrimp paste can be used straight from the packet if it is to be ground with other herbs and spices and fried, but it should be toasted or baked to temper its raw taste before using in sambals, dressings and salads.

1 Cut off a small lump of shrimp paste and shape it into a 1cm/½in cube. Mould the paste on to the end of a long metal skewer.

2 Rotate the cube over a low to medium flame, or under an electric grill (broiler), until it begins to char a little along the edges. Ventilate your kitchen to let the strong smell dissipate as it can linger.

3 Alternatively, wrap the paste in a piece of foil and heat in a pan, turning occasionally, or wrap it in a microwavable, ventilated bag and microwave for 20–30 seconds.

POULTRY

Singapore, having no poultry industry at all, imports all its birds from Malaysia and the neighbouring countries. There is a thriving poultry industry in Malaysia, but some birds are imported from neighbouring countries such as Thailand, Burma and Vietnam and some from Hong Kong.

Chicken is popular among the Chinese community as it symbolizes prosperity and abundance and it is always the featured dish during Chinese New Year and at wedding feasts. Newly married couples are supposed to place a rooster and a hen under their nuptial bed to see which one emerges first. The gender of the first emerging bird is supposed to predict the sex of the firstborn child.

In Singapore, chicken and duck are staple fare, featuring in well-known dishes such as Hainanese chicken rice and Cantonese duck rice. Both birds are frequently roasted, soy braised or barbecued.

CHICKEN

Chickens in South-east Asia are mostly battery-reared today in Singapore and are mainly bought from supermarkets. Free-range birds are more expensive and apart from those bred by rural families they do not feature very much in either cuisine.

There is a breed of black-skinned chicken that practitioners of traditional Chinese medicine advocate eating to alleviate menstrual problems. These chickens taste exactly like any other but are said to contain high levels of an antioxidant. They are not easy to find, but can be bought in some specialist Chinese shops.

DUCK

As with chicken, duck-rearing is confined to rural communities of Malaysia and neighbouring countries, but many are imported into Singapore from China and Thailand. As it is a tough bird to cook, duck is used in relatively few dishes, such as roast duck, soy-braised duck, Nonya duck and salted vegetable soup and coriander-braised duck.

GOOSE

This is not a common bird in Singapore, but the Teochews excel at cooking geese. In a few restaurants in Singapore and Kuala Lumpur, the large bird is braised in a rich broth of soy sauce, sugar, five-spice powder and galangal called *siew ngor*. It is then sliced and served with a sharp chilli and vinegar sauce and plain rice. Geese are commercially rare and have to be ordered specially from supermarkets.

PIGEON AND QUAIL

Small birds, such as quail and squab, are uncommon, but quails' eggs are sold widely in Chinese stores. They usually end up in soups. The birds used to be popular Chinese restaurant items but have become very rare. They are best marinated in wine and soy sauce and deep-fried. In each case, the birds are killed and then plunged into boiling water to make the feathers easier to pull off. They are then gutted, and the blood and offal are reserved for special dishes. There is little wastage of any bird, fish or animal, especially in Chinese kitchens.

Above: Grilled chickens. Much poultry is sold with its head intact, according to local custom. Western food regulations generally prohibit this practice.

EGG

Almost all eggs are edible, and around the world eggs of all types of birds are farmed. Hens' eggs are mainstream items. Duck eggs, on the other hand, are rare and are usually only available salted or as century eggs, which are a special treat eaten with pickled ginger.

Chinese in origin, salted duck eggs are boiled and eaten with rice congee, or in the Singapore dish of oyster omelette that can be found in every food court and hawker centre. The eggs are salted by steeping them in salty water or brine for a few weeks. When boiled, their whites turn opaque and the yolks brilliant orange.

Century eggs are made by coating eggs with a paste made of alkaline clay and rice husks and keeping them in a dark place for several weeks (but not a hundred years) until their whites turn dark brown and their yolks a dull grey, with a creamy texture and a flavour rather like cheese.

MEAT

In Singapore only 20 per cent of the population are Muslims, unlike Malaysia, which is a predominantly Muslim country with some 80 per cent of the people observing Islam. The remainder of the population in both countries is a mix of Chinese, Indians, Eurasians and other migrant races. The types of meat eaten tend to be related to the restrictions of Islam, Hinduism and Buddhism. Among the Christians and Taoists in the region there are fewer taboos affecting the eating of meat.

Muslims eschew pork, and Hindus and devout Buddhists do not eat beef. For this reason, pork is more popular in Singapore than in Malaysia. Mutton is more popular among Indians as both beef and lamb, being imported meats, can be expensive.

Although there are some pig farms in Malaysia, run by Chinese, most of the pork eaten in the region tends to be imported from Thailand and Vietnam, or from Australia, even further afield. Being almost completely urbanized, Singapore imports all its meat.

BEEF, LAMB AND MUTTON

An expensive meat in Asia, beef is eaten as a special treat, mainly in restaurant dishes. Beef satay is quite popular in Singapore, but the meat is more often than not taken from cheaper cuts, which are tenderized to make the spicy skewers.

The lamb dishes eaten in the two countries mainly originate from North China. The meat, being imported from Australia or New Zealand, is usually reserved for special occasions or eaten in restaurant dishes. Where you see lamb satay on a menu, they are invariably made of mutton, which is more readily available in South-east Asia and therefore cheaper.

WILD BOAR

This is an delicious meat that can be found only in select areas such as Johor and Kuala Lumpur. It is sourced from rural areas of Malaysia where the animal still thrives in the wild and imported into Singapore. Wild boar roasted with spices makes a tasty dish.

PORK

Chinese cooks have many ways to cook pork but the distinctive feature of their cookery lies in the way the pork is cut and sold, which is entirely different from western practice. Leg of pork is preferred for stews, belly for stock, stir-fries and the famous Nonya spiced roast pork (*babi panggang*). Fillets are generally roasted for banquets and wedding feasts, and suckling pig is a premium restaurant offering. Trotters are popular, ending up in soy sauce stews or slow-cooked in soups. Virtually every part of the pig is eaten and offal (variety meat) is popular despite its high cholesterol content. Foreign visitors are often amused by (and sometimes brave enough to eat) a popular Singapore dish called pig's organ soup, which features practically every part of the animal.

Probably the most high-profile and universally loved pork dish is *char siew*, or Cantonese roast pork, which goes into many dishes, including roast pork rice, a lunchtime staple in Singapore and Malaysia, *kon lo mee* (Cantonese roast pork noodles, *char siew bau* (dumplings) and *bak chang* (Nonya glutinous rice dumplings).

Minced pork

Minced (ground) pork is used for meatballs and fillings and added to porridge for late-night supper dishes.

Pork and liver sausages are mainly imported from China and are used in Cantonese dishes such as fried rice and dumplings. Pork hams are relatively rare and come mostly from the province of Hunan. These can be expensive and are used sparingly in festive soups and banquet dishes.

Barbecued pork

All over Singapore, and to a lesser extent in Kuala Lumpur and Penang, you can find stalls barbecuing thin slices of highly seasoned pork, which has become a national dish. The strips are given away at Chinese New Year as symbolic gifts and many a Singaporean would not travel overseas without a kilo or so of this special treat.

Preserved pork

Also called wind-dried pork, these strips of pork, usually cut from the belly, are highly seasoned and generally cooked in braised dishes. Some offal, such as liver and tripe, is dried or preserved for soups and stews.

Left: Meats are often marinated to tenderize and infuse them with flavour.

HERBS AND SPICES

Herbs and spices are integral to all Asian cooking, ground up in complex blends or used as top notes in curries, soups and stir-fries. They play a fundamental role in Singaporean cuisines, particularly in those of the Malay, Indian and Peranakan communities. Within the range of dried whole and ground spices and fresh herbs, the varieties are endless. Subtle, pungent or heady fresh herbs such as basil, lemon grass, coriander (cilantro), mint, chillies, lime leaves, chives, pandan and other esoterics are even reputed to have medicinal and restorative properties.

Dried ground spices such as coriander, cumin, fenugreek, aniseed, turmeric and chilli all find a place within the spectrum of spicy cooking. Other flavouring ingredients include tamarind both fresh and dried, in pastes and concentrates, sesame seeds, dried lily buds, sugar cane, palm sugar and limes. It is important to remember that, when using herbs for the preparation of curry pastes and sambals, it is not an exact science. The alchemy between the ingredients is often unfathomable but works brilliantly.

Many of the spices and herbs used in the region have been around for centuries, since the Portuguese first came to the seaport of Melaka, bringing with them many unheard-of ingredients from South and Central America. Today they are grown in every home vegetable plot, on market farms, hillsides and in backyards. Indeed, many a dish would be a pale shadow of itself but for a herb or two, chopped, torn or added to curries at the last minute to impart their unique, evocative perfumes.

LAKSA LEAVES

With the botanical name of *Polygonum*, this fragrant leaf was adopted by Singaporeans as an essential ingredient in laksa, earning it the name "laksa leaf". The small, thin leaves jutting from slender stalks have a distinct lemony perfume with hints of coriander, mint and basil. A variety grown in Vietnam, where it is called *rau rum*, is also known as Vietnamese coriander or mint.

LIME LEAVES

Also known as kaffir lime leaves (limau perut-Malay), these are unique to the South-east Asian culinary heritage. Grown widely in all tropical regions, the plant is used mainly for its leaves which have a distinctive citrus perfume when crushed. Each leaf is shaped like a guitar or figure eight. The fruit is walnut–sized with a knobbly green skin.

MINT

The most commonly used mint is similar to the garden mint of the West, with furry leaves and a sweet flavour. It is used in salads and as a garnish, often with basil and coriander. There are numerous varieties, including spearmint and peppermint, differing widely in size, shape and flavour.

PANDAN LEAF

One of the most popular herbs in Malaysian and Singaporean cooking, pandan leaves grow like weeds in tropical Asia, and the plant from which they

Above: Holy basil is quite pungent with an almost spicy taste.

come is also known as the screwpine. Used as much for their green colouring as for their perfume, pandan leaves impart a distinctive, vanilla-like scent to puddings. The long, narrow leaves are knotted or bruised to release their unique flavour before being added to dishes. They are also used as a natural wrapper for poultry, meat and seafood for deep frying. The leaves are available fresh or dried in some Asian markets. Some stores also stock pandan essence but if you can't find either, you could use vanilla pods (beans) instead.

BASIL

The basil family is diverse, encompassing different shapes, sizes, colours and aromatic nuances. The types most commonly found in Asia are Thai sweet basil, holy basil and lemon basil. Called *daun selasih* in Malay, Thai sweet basil has the broadest range. Aromatic and reminiscent of anise, it is mild enough to be eaten as a vegetable. In Malay and Nonya cooking, basil is always used raw, sprinkled on noodle soups, tossed in salads or added to curries. Asian basil is found in Asian markets, but the sweet Mediterranean basil found in all supermarkets can be used as a substitute.

Left: Coriander (cilantro) leaves are used to flavour many savoury dishes and as a popular garnish.

CHIVES

Across Asia, chives are found in three forms: green chives, with flat stems and slim-bladed leaves; yellow chives, which are the same variety grown under a cloche, which explains their pallor; and flowering chives, whose round stems are tipped by pointed pale green flower buds. All have a mild spring onion (scallions) flavour with a hint of garlic.

CORIANDER (CILANTRO)

Ubiquitous in most tropical and temperate countries, originally from Central Asia, coriander is the most common culinary herb, and its seeds are ground into powder as a key ingredient in curries. The feathery, citrus-flavoured leaves are used liberally, especially in soups, Chinese noodle dishes, dumpling mixes and garnishes. Bunches of fresh leaves are available in Asian stores and supermarkets.

Preparing dried chillies

1 Remove the stems and seeds with a knife. Cut into pieces and place in a bowl.

2 Pour over hot water and leave to soak for about 30 minutes. Drain and use according to the recipe.

Right: Red and green Thai bird's eye chillies.

CURRY LEAVES

Very much an Indian herb, curry leaves are diamond-shaped, tough, bottle green and hang in even rows from thin stems. They have a warm peppery scent with citrus notes when crushed and add a distinct flavour to seafood curries, chutneys, rasams (sour soups) and relishes.

CHILLIES

Both fresh and dried chillies are used generously in Malay, Indian and Nonya cooking. Most pastes use dried chillies as they have a more intense red colour, while fresh chillies are the norm for delicate seafood curries, salads and in dips with soy sauce. There are many types of chillies, with fire ranging from barely there to flaming inferno. Green ones are often eaten raw like a vegetable.

Thai bird chillies

These tiny pods have a fire that is disproportionate to their size. They come in many colours, ranging from pale yellow to green, orange and bright red, and are best de-seeded as it is the seeds and pithy flesh around them that are overpoweringly hot. Only two or three are sufficient to give incendiary fire to curries and soups. Thai bird chillies are available fresh and dried in Asian stores and from most supermarkets.

Dried chillies

Also used to make chilli oil, dried chillies are made by infusing them in palm or grape seed oil. Dried chillies can be bought, whole or chopped, from Asian stores and some supermarkets. For most complex curry pastes, they are preferable to fresh chillies. If kept in a dry, cool place, dried chillies have a long shelf life.

Right: Dried chillies.

Preparing fresh chillies

An ingredient called capsaicin found in the seeds and pith gives chillies their fire. Bird chillies can be so hot as to give a burning sensation when merely touched. Always wash your hands after preparing them, or wear gloves.

Slice the chilli in half and run the blade of the knife from stalk to tip to remove all the hottest parts. To seed a chilli without splitting it, slice off the stalk and roll the chilli between your finger and thumb. Hold the chilli upside-down and shake it to release the seeds.

CHILLI PRODUCTS

Sauces and oils made with chilli are great for adding a dash of fire to all kinds of savoury dishes.

Chilli powder

This deep-red powder is made by finely grinding dried red chillies. Any chilli can be used but the hottest powder is made from dried Thai bird chillies.

Chilli paste

This is made by grinding red chillies, seeded or otherwise, into a fine paste. You may add ground garlic, ginger or aromatics depending on what the paste is to be used for. Oil is added if you want a smooth consistency. Versatile and popular, it is used to season sauces, added to curry pastes or as a condiment to salads, relishes and dips for fried snacks. Ready-made chilli paste is sold in jars in Asian markets.

Chilli sauce

This is a smooth, potent sauce used as a dipping sauce on its own, or splashed into fried noodles or *nasi goreng* (Malay fried rice). Many brands are widely available from Asian markets and supermarkets, some with garlic or ginger purée added.

Chilli oil

Used to enhance the colour and flavour of curries, laksas and spicy soups, chilli oil can be made by infusing whole dried chillies, or chilli flakes, in grape seed or palm oil. Heat the oil gently in a very clean pan and infuse the chillies for a few minutes, then strain and store in a glass jar or bottle.

CARDAMOM

Grown widely in the Middle East, India and Nepal, cardamoms come in two varieties – large black and small green pods. They play an important role as a peppery note in rice dishes, soups and curries. Black cardamoms are used sparingly as they are hard to come by. Green cardamoms are added whole to a range of curries but must be discarded before serving as they are not edible, only used for their spicy aroma.

Above: Dried tiger lily buds must be soaked for 30 minutes.

CHINESE FIVE-SPICE POWDER

Based on a mixture of five spices – star anise, cloves, fennel seeds, cinnamon and Sichuan peppercorns – five-spice powder is designed to be pungent. It is used sparingly, mostly in spring roll fillings or in stewed pork dishes, to which it adds a unique flavour. The mixture correlates to the five different types of flavour traditionally said to be at the heart of Chinese cooking – sweet, sour, bitter, hot and salty. In traditional Chinese medicine five-spice powder is often used in relation to the five major organs of the human body – heart, lungs, liver, kidney and spleen. Five-spice powder is widely available.

CINNAMON

A member of the cassia family, the cinnamon tree is grown widely in the Himalayas, Sri Lanka, China and South-east Asia. The most common bark used is that of the Chinese cinnamon, which is thick, rich in oils and a deep brown colour. A warm and pungent ingredient with constituents of volatile oil, cinnamon is added to traditional soups and rice dishes and some cakes, either powdered or in sticks of curled bark. It is available in most Asian stores and supermarkets.

CLOVES

This spice has been known worldwide since the fifth century. In India, cloves are chewed with betel leaves as a digestive aid. They are used primarily as a culinary spice to perfume soups, cakes and stews. They have a warm, spicy aroma and liquorice flavour and are widely available in most Indian stores and supermarkets.

LILY BUDS

Native to Asia, lily buds from the tiger lily plant are prized for their colour and texture in Chinese vegetarian dishes, but are also used in Nonya soups and braised dishes. Bags of dried, tangled buds are sold in Asian markets. They will keep almost indefinitely if stored in an airtight container, away from strong light, heat or moisture. Also known as golden needles, they are light golden in colour. Crunchy in texture, lily buds are floral-scented and earthy in flavour with mushroom overtones.

Preparing lily buds

1 Remove the woody tips of the stems with a sharp knife.

2 Knot the buds in the centre and soak in water for about 30 minutes, then drain and rinse in cold water until clean. This ensures that the lilies remain intact when cooked and retain a slightly chewy texture.

Above: Star-shaped star anise is often used to infuse stocks and medicinal teas.

SESAME SEEDS

These tiny white or black seeds are commonly used in many Chinese dishes. They have a subtle nutty flavour and are most often used to coat meats for deep frying, or sprinkled on stir-fries. Ground up and cooked with sugar as a thick gruel, sesame seeds make a favourite late-night snack.

STAR ANISE

Also known as Chinese anise, this is the dried, star-shaped fruit of a slender evergreen tree that grows in China, India and Japan, where the bark is ground to powder and burnt as incense in temples. Not related to aniseed, star anise imparts a strong liquorice flavour and is generally used in tandem with cloves in aromatic soups and curries. Whole, or crushed, star anise is one of the principal ingredients in five-spice powder. It is available whole or ground from all Asian stores.

GARLIC

Highly prized for more than 5,000 years, garlic is a member of the lily family. Each bulb may contain up to

Above: Cloves of fresh and dried garlic vary in pungency.

10 cloves, which should be firm with a pungent aroma and flavour. Chopped or crushed, garlic is fried in oil to impart flavour to stir-fries, curries, stews and noodles. It is also used in its raw form to flavour pickles, marinades, sauces and dips. Garlic is believed to be good for the heart and circulation.

GALANGAL

While it is a member of the ginger family and similar in appearance, galangal is never eaten raw, unlike ginger itself. The aroma and distinctive pungency of galangal are best harnessed in tandem with shallots, garlic and chillies in spice pastes and marinades. The rhizomes can be sliced or bruised and added to soups and curries to impart a more subtle flavour. When young they are creamy pink in colour with a lemony flavour; the more mature ones are golden and peppery. Fresh galangal will keep for about one week if it is sealed in a plastic bag and refrigerated. It can also be frozen. Both dried and bottled galangal purée are available from Asian stores. Another good way to keep it is to plant it in a pot of moist earth, where it will stay fresh for weeks and may even reward you by starting to grow after a few months.

Above: Beneficial in cooking as well as in the spirit world, garlic is used liberally in South-east Asian dishes.

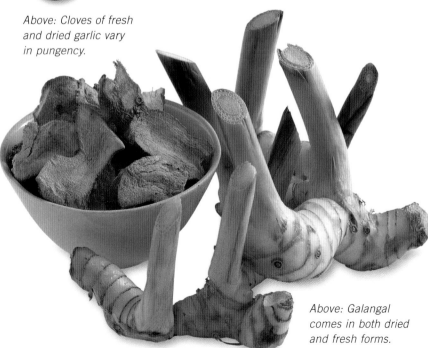

Above: Galangal comes in both dried and fresh forms.

Below: Fresh root ginger, ginger paste and ground ginger.

Above: Ground and fresh turmeric.

dishes. Pale yellowish-green in colour, the paper-like sheath that encases the stem has to be removed before use. The root end is chopped, pounded or crushed before being added to spice blends, stir-fries, curries and marinades. Lemon grass is one of the principal flavouring ingredients in Malay and Nonya cooking and is available both fresh and dried from Asian stores and some supermarkets.

SHALLOTS

These small, marble-sized bulbs form the sweet basis of many spice blends and when fried in oil make a crunchy garnish in many Malay soups. Spring onions (scallions), which are the young stems of shallots, appear in many dishes. They are often chopped and used liberally as a garnish, added to Chinese spring rolls and tossed into stir-fries at the last minute.

TURMERIC

The fresh root has a subtle, earthy taste and imparts its vivid colour and flavour to spice blends. It is also dried and ground to a deep-yellow powder which imparts colour with only the slightest hint of flavour. Both fresh and dried turmeric are available in Asian markets.

Left: Fresh lemon grass stalks.

GINGER

Indigenous to most of South-east Asia, ginger is the oldest and most widely used flavouring across the Asian region, especially in Indian and Indonesian cooking. A herbaceous perennial plant, root ginger, which is actually a rhizome, is knobbly-looking with a smooth, beige skin. It is sold in two forms. Young, pale yellow ginger is fresh-looking and tender, with a slightly sweet pungency. It can be chopped or shredded for stir-fries, stews, rice, pickles, steamed dishes and puddings. Older, fibrous pieces of ginger are usually ground into spice blends or pickled to make relish.

Ginger is well documented in both traditional Chinese medicine and Indian Ayurvedic practice for its carminative and expectorant action. It is also believed to help with motion sickness and bronchial problems. Choose smooth, plump, fresh-looking pieces and store them in a cool, dry place.

GINKGO NUTS

Also known as the maidenhair tree, the ginkgo plant dates back some two million years. Native to Japan and the central Chinese provinces, ginkgo nuts are used in stir-fries, as a soup ingredient and in desserts, usually in combination with lotus seeds. They have a mild nutty flavour and are available fresh or canned in most Asian stores and health food shops.

LEMON GRASS

A woody, fibrous stalk, lemon grass transcends all South-east Asian culinary cultures. It imparts a fragrant, citrus flavour to

STORE-CUPBOARD INGREDIENTS

A wide range of flavoured oils and sauces are found in Singaporean kitchens, together with staple ingredients such as sugar, salt, agar agar and peanuts.

SESAME OIL

Extracted from sesame seeds, this oil is commonly used in stir-fried dishes. Two types are available: the plain, pale golden oil, which is mildly nutty and good for frying; and the darker, richer-tasting oil made from roasted sesame seeds, which is usually added to dishes in small quantities for flavour just before serving.

FISH SAUCE

More usually associated with Thai cooking, fish sauce is an essential ingredient in some curries, dips and stir fries. Despite its pungent smell, it imparts a superb flavour. Bottles of the sauce, which is made from fermented fish or shrimp, may be kept for up to a year once opened as long as they are kept in a cool, dark place.

ANCHOVY SAUCE

Chinese in origin, this pungent, salty sauce is often used in combination with a sweet, fruity ingredient, such as ripe pineapple. Bottles of this thick, light-grey sauce can be found in Asian stores and markets.

OYSTER SAUCE

This thick, brown sauce is made from dried oyster extract, sugar, water and salt. Strongly flavoured and salty, it is used in moderation as a seasoning agent in Chinese-style dishes. It is available in Asian stores.

HOISIN SAUCE

This is a thick, sweet bean sauce of Chinese origin. Primarily made from fermented soya beans, vinegar, sugar and five-spice powder, it is rich in flavour and ideal for marinades and dipping sauces. It is also used to season noodle soups. Bottles of hoisin sauce are available in most supermarkets.

SOY SAUCE

Probably the most commonly used sauce in South-east Asia is soy sauce, in its various guises, which is made from fermented soya beans, wheat and yeast, Naturally fermented soy sauce will not keep forever; it starts to lose its flavour as soon as the bottle is opened. Try to use it up fairly quickly. Essential to cuisines in Asia, such as Malay and Chinese cuisines, it has also been adopted by Indian cooks who use it to make sweet, spicy sauces for meat stews and curries.

CHINESE WINE

Two types of wine are commonly used in Chinese cooking, called Hsiao Hsing and Hua Teow wines. They are similar in flavour and are used to souse rich stews and stir-fries in northern Chinese cooking. They are made from grain such as sorghum, millet and rye, not from grapes. Cooking sherry makes a decent substitute.

FERMENTED SOYA BEANS

Sometimes called salted beans, this is a condiment (*tuong hot*) made from whole beans. It is used mainly in Chinese-style dishes as a seasoning ingredient.

Left: Oyster sauce.

Right: Palm sugar is sold in blocks, which store well in a cool, dry place.

Right: Toasted sesame oil imparts a rich flavour to many dishes.

PALM SUGAR (JAGGERY)

Widely used in South-east Asia, palm sugar is extracted from the sap of various palm trees. The sap is collected from incisions made in the trunks of the trees. Palm sugar is golden to toffee-brown in colour with a distinctive flavour. It is usually sold in blocks, often referred to as jaggery in Asian stores.

SAMBAL GORENG (FRIED CHILLI PASTE)

Unlike basic chilli paste, this is a master sauce that Singaporean kitchens are rarely without. It goes into a range of dishes, from noodles and rice to curries and salads.

Preparing sambal goreng

250g/9oz onions
50g/2oz garlic
15–20 dried chillies, or to taste
40g/1½oz shrimp paste
100ml/3½oz/scant ½ cup
  vegetable oil
25g/1oz tomato purée (paste)
5ml/1 tsp salt
5ml/1 tsp sugar or to taste
30ml/2 tbsp tamarind concentrate

1 Grind the first four ingredients until fine and fry for 10 minutes.

2 Add tomato purée, salt, sugar and tamarind and cook for 2 minutes. Remove and store for up to 2 weeks in a refrigerator, in a tightly-sealed container.

SALT

This simple ingredient is one of the most widely used in the world. The sea is the main source of salt in South-east Asia, but salty-flavoured soy sauce and fish sauces often replace it as a seasoning in cooking. Salt is combined in equal amounts with pepper to season deep-fried prawns (shrimp) and squid. It is also commonly used as a last-minute seasoning. Mixed with Chinese five-spice powder, or chilli powder, a salt dip is often on the table for roasted or grilled (broiled) meat and poultry or to sprinkle over a meat stew.

AGAR AGAR

Similar to gelatine, agar agar is a gum that is extracted from dried seaweed and processed into white sticks, or ground to a powder. Once dissolved in boiling water, it turns to jelly and is widely used in the jellied puddings of South-east Asia.

Right (clockwise from bottom right): Agar agar is sold in thick and thin strips and as a powder that is used as a setting agent.

PEANUTS

Important in Singaporean cuisine, peanuts are used for richness and texture in a variety of dishes. They are sprinkled on salads and are key to the sauces for *rojak* and *satay*, in which ground peanuts thicken a spicy mix of coconut milk, onions, garlic, shrimp paste and lemon grass.

TAMARIND

The tamarind tree is cultivated in India, South-east Asia and the West Indies. The sticky, tartly flavoured flesh of the tamarind pod is an important flavouring in Indian and Asian cooking. It is strained to remove the seeds and fibrous threads and the resulting paste is available in jars and blocks from Asian markets and supermarkets.

Below: Peanuts are sometimes roasted and crushed for use as a garnish.

Preparing tamarind from paste

Many recipes from Singapore will call for tamarind, so it is worth obtaining tamarind block and having it as a store-cupboard staple. You will need warm water and a nylon sieve (strainer) to prepare it.

1 Crumble 300g/11oz of the block and mix with 500ml/17fl oz/ 2 generous cups water. Strain through a fine sieve to obtain a sour, dark brown liquid.

2 Add as much tamarind solution as taste dictates to fish and shellfish curries.

The thick tamarind concentrate can be used straight from the jar or can, again depending on taste. Use it sparingly at first.

BROTHS AND SOUPY NOODLES

Steaming bowls of fragrant, clear broth brimming with noodles, vegetables, succulent seafood and tender meat are the staple fare of hawker stalls and coffee shops in Singapore. They make sustaining lunches and late-night snacks. Years ago, itinerant hawkers used to roam the streets carrying a pole laden with two baskets: one held a stove and a cooking pot, the other held the ingredients for the soup, which could be quickly rustled up for hungry customers.

TAMARIND <u>AND</u> PRAWN SOUP

THIS IS A HYBRID DISH SPANNING INDIAN AND THAI TRADITIONS AND LIBERALLY TWEAKED BY NONYA COOKS, WHO PREFER TO LEAVE PRAWNS IN THEIR SHELLS. TAMARIND PLAYS A KEY ROLE IN ASIAN FOOD, MUCH LIKE LEMON JUICE IN THE WEST. IT USED TO BE SOLD IN NEAR-SOLID BLOCKS FULL OF PIPS AND GRIT, BUT THE MODERN CONCENTRATE NEEDS NO STRAINING AND IS READY TO USE.

SERVES TWO

INGREDIENTS
    6 raw tiger prawns (jumbo shrimp)
    600ml/1 pint/2½ cups water
    30g/2 tbsp tamarind concentrate
    15ml/1 tbsp fish sauce
    5ml/1 tsp sugar
    chopped spring onions (scallions)
      to garnish
For the spice paste
    2 red chillies
    15g/½oz fresh turmeric, peeled
    ½ large onion
    2 garlic cloves
    1 lemon grass stalk, 7.5cm/3in of
      root end only

1 Wash the prawns in cold, fresh water and snip about 1cm/½in of the head and the feelers off with scissors, but leave the shells on. Pat the prawns dry with kitchen towels and set aside in a cool place.

2 Grind the ingredients for the spice paste together until very fine, using a mortar and pestle or a food processor. Blend the water and tamarind concentrate, then bring to the boil in a small pan. Add the spice paste.

3 Simmer for 3 minutes, then add the prawns. Season with the fish sauce and sugar. Cook for about 5 minutes or until the prawns have turned completely pink. Serve immediately, garnished with chopped spring onions.

COOK'S TIP
Leaving the prawns in their shells gives the best flavour, but shelling them makes the soup easier to eat. If you prefer to peel the prawns before cooking, add shells to the pan in step 3, then strain the soup and discard the shells before adding the peeled prawns. This will enrich the flavour of the soup.

Per portion Energy 92kcal/387kJ; Protein 14.2g; Carbohydrate 6.1g, of which sugars 6g; Fat 1.3g, of which saturates 0.3g; Cholesterol 48mg; Calcium 122mg; Fibre 0.8g; Sodium 1627mg.

SINGAPORE LAKSA

THERE ARE AS MANY LAKSA DISHES AS THERE ARE DIVERSE REGIONS IN SINGAPORE. THE BASIC DISH CONSISTS OF NOODLES IN A SPICY COCONUT BROTH. IN THE HOME-COOKED SINGAPORE LAKSA, SLICES OF DEEP-FRIED FISH CAKES ARE OFTEN ADDED AT THE END, WHEREAS THE STALL VERSION IS RICH IN A VARIETY OF SEAFOOD, TOPPED WITH COCKLES.

SERVES FOUR TO SIX

INGREDIENTS

For the spice paste
8 shallots, chopped
4 garlic cloves, chopped
40g/1½oz fresh root ginger, peeled and chopped
2 lemon grass stalks, chopped
6 candlenuts or macadamia nuts
4 dried red chillies, soaked until soft and seeded
30ml/2 tbsp dried prawns (shrimp), soaked until soft
5–10ml/1–2 tsp belacan
5–10ml/1–2 tsp sugar
15ml/1 tbsp vegetable oil

For the laksa
vegetable oil, for deep-frying
6 shallots, finely sliced
600ml/1 pint/2½ cups coconut milk
400ml/14fl oz/1⅔ cups chicken stock
90g/3½oz prawns (shrimp), shelled
90g/3½oz squid, cleaned, trimmed and sliced
6–8 scallops
75g/3oz cockles, shelled
225g/8oz fresh rice noodles or dried rice vermicelli, soaked in lukewarm water until pliable
90g/3½oz beansprouts
salt and ground black pepper
a small bunch of Vietnamese mint or fresh garden mint, roughly chopped, and chilli oil, to garnish

1 Using a mortar and pestle or food processor, grind all the ingredients for the spice paste mixture, apart from the oil. Add the oil to the paste to bind it and set aside.

2 Heat the oil for deep-frying in a wok. Add the sliced shallots to the oil and deep-fry until crispy and golden. Drain and set aside.

3 Heat 30ml/2 tbsp vegetable oil in a large wok or heavy pan. Stir in the spice paste and cook over a low heat for 3–4 minutes, until fragrant.

4 Add the coconut milk and chicken stock and bring to the boil, stirring all the time. Add the prawns, squid and scallops and simmer gently for 5–10 minutes, until the seafood is cooked. Add the cockles at the last minute and season the broth with salt and pepper.

5 Ladle the noodles into individual bowls. Add the beansprouts and ladle over the broth and seafood, making sure the noodles are submerged in the steaming liquid. Garnish the bowls with the crispy shallots, mint and a drizzle of chilli oil.

Per Portion Energy 300Kcal/1254kJ; Protein 14.2g; Carbohydrate 38g, of which sugars 6.9g; Fat 10.3g, of which saturates 1.4g; Cholesterol 77mg; Calcium 69mg; Fibre 0.7g; Sodium 211mg.

MOOLI AND PRAWN SOUP

THIS VERY SIMPLE SOUP OF CANTONESE ORIGIN IS OFTEN DRUNK AS A COOLING BREW TO COUNTERACT A SURFEIT OF SPICY DISHES. MOOLI IS FULL OF FLAVOUR AND HAS AN IMPORTANT PLACE WITHIN THE RANGE OF CHINESE YIN FOODS PURPORTED TO DISPEL BODY HEAT.

SERVES FOUR

INGREDIENTS
    150g/5oz mooli (daikon), peeled
    700ml/1¼ pints/2¾ cups water
    5ml/1 tsp salt
    15ml/1 tbsp sesame oil
    115g/4oz prawns (shrimp), shelled
    1 spring onion (scallion), trimmed
      and chopped
    freshly ground black pepper

COOK'S TIP
Mooli is the Hindi name for the large
white radish or daikon.

1 Slice the mooli into thin matchstick
pieces. Bring water to the boil, add the
mooli, salt and sesame oil and simmer
for 15 minutes.

2 Add the prawns and simmer for
5 minutes. Scatter with chopped spring
onion, add black pepper to taste and
serve immediately.

Per portion Energy 52kcal/215kJ; Protein 5.4g; Carbohydrate 0.8g, of which sugars 0.8g; Fat 3g, of which saturates 0.5g; Cholesterol 56mg; Calcium 31mg; Fibre 0.4g; Sodium 550mg.

HOT AND SOUR PINEAPPLE PRAWN BROTH

THIS SIMPLE NONYA DISH IS SERVED AS AN APPETITE ENHANCER BECAUSE OF ITS HOT AND SOUR FLAVOUR. IT IS ALSO POPULAR AS AN ACCOMPANIMENT TO PLAIN RICE OR NOODLES. IN SOME RESTAURANTS, THE BROTH IS PRESENTED IN A HOLLOWED-OUT PINEAPPLE, HALVED LENGTHWAYS.

SERVES FOUR

INGREDIENTS
    30ml/2 tbsp vegetable oil
    15–30ml/1–2 tbsp tamarind
        paste
    15ml/1 tbsp sugar
    450g/1lb raw prawns (shrimp),
        peeled and deveined
    4 thick fresh pineapple slices, cored
        and cut into bitesize chunks
    salt and ground black pepper
    fresh coriander (cilantro) and mint
        leaves, to garnish
    steamed rice or plain noodles,
        to serve
For the spice paste
    4 shallots, chopped
    4 red chillies, chopped
    25g/1oz fresh root ginger, peeled
        and chopped
    1 lemon grass stalk, trimmed and
        chopped
    5ml/1 tsp shrimp paste

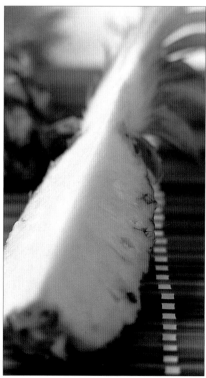

1 Grind the shallots, chillies, ginger and lemon grass to a paste. Add the shrimp paste and mix well.

2 Heat the oil in a wok or heavy pan. Stir in the spice paste and fry until fragrant. Stir in the tamarind paste and the sugar, then pour in 1.2 litres/2 pints/5 cups water. Mix well and bring to the boil. Reduce the heat and simmer for 10 minutes. Season the broth with salt and pepper.

3 Add the prawns and pineapple to the broth and simmer for 4–5 minutes, or until the prawns are cooked. Using a slotted spoon, lift the prawns and pineapple out of the broth and divide them among four warmed bowls. Ladle over some of the broth and garnish with coriander and mint leaves. The remaining broth can be served separately as a drink, or spooned over steamed rice or plain noodles, if they are accompanying this dish.

Per Portion Energy 192Kcal/808kJ; Protein 20.4g; Carbohydrate 14.2g, of which sugars 13.9g; Fat 6.4g, of which saturates 0.8g; Cholesterol 219mg; Calcium 111mg; Fibre 1.3g; Sodium 216mg.

HOKKIEN PRAWN NOODLE SOUP

INTRODUCED TO SINGAPORE BY THE CHINESE FROM FUJIAN, HOKKIEN NOODLE SOUP, KNOWN AS HAY MEE, IS SOLD AT THE HAWKER STALLS AND IN THE COFFEE SHOPS. AS MOST OF THE CHINESE POPULATION OF SINGAPORE IS HOKKIEN, IT IS AN ENDURINGLY POPULAR DISH THERE.

1 Put all the stock ingredients into a deep pan along with the prawn shells. Pour in 2 litres/3½ pints/7¾ cups water and bring to the boil. Reduce the heat and simmer gently, uncovered, for about 2 hours, until the stock has reduced by half.

2 Strain the stock into a clean pan and put it over a low heat to keep hot. Season with salt and pepper to taste.

3 In a small pan heat the sugar with 15ml/1 tbsp water. Stir over a low heat until the sugar dissolves, then boil without stirring until it turns a rich brown. Add it to the stock and mix well.

4 Cut the bacon into 1cm/½in slices. In a heavy pan, dry-fry the bacon until it turns crispy and golden. Drain on kitchen paper and set aside.

5 Using a perforated ladle or sieve (strainer), plunge the noodles into the hot stock for 1 minute to heat through, then divide them among four bowls. Add the prawns to the stock, heat for 1 minute, remove with a slotted spoon and add to the bowls.

6 Add the beansprouts to the prawns and noodles and ladle the hot stock into the bowls. Scatter the crispy bacon and spring onions over the top and serve the soup immediately in warmed bowls.

SERVES FOUR TO SIX

INGREDIENTS
For the stock
  45ml/3 tbsp dried shrimp
  1 dried red chilli
  50g/2oz fresh root ginger, peeled
   and sliced
  2 onions, quartered
  4 garlic cloves, bruised
  2 lemon grass stalks, bruised
  2.5ml/½ tsp black peppercorns
  30–45ml/2–3 tbsp dark soy sauce
  700g/1lb 10oz pork and chicken bones

For the soup
  15ml/1 tbsp sugar
  6 rashers (strips) streaky
   (fatty) bacon
  150g/5oz fresh egg noodles
  20 fresh, large prawns (shrimp),
   peeled (keep the shells to one
   side to add to the stock)
  90g/3½oz beansprouts
  2 spring onions (scallions), trimmed
   and finely sliced
  salt and ground black pepper

Per Portion Energy 257Kcal/1082kJ; Protein 18.7g; Carbohydrate 27.1g, of which sugars 6.9g; Fat 9g, of which saturates 2.8g; Cholesterol 94mg; Calcium 145mg; Fibre 3g; Sodium 1080mg.

SPICY CHICKEN SOUP

THIS FRAGRANT SOUP IS PARTICULARLY POPULAR IN SINGAPORE. ORIGINALLY FROM JAVA, VARIOUS VERSIONS ARE SERVED AT SOUP AND NOODLE STALLS SPECIALIZING IN INDONESIAN AND MALAY FOOD. WHEN SERVED AS A MEAL ON ITS OWN, DEEP-FRIED POTATO FRITTERS OR CHIPS ARE ADDED.

SERVES SIX

INGREDIENTS
  1 small chicken, about 900g/2lb
  2 lemon grass stalks, bruised
  25g/1oz fresh root ginger, peeled
    and sliced
  2 fresh kaffir lime leaves
  1 dried red chilli
  30ml/2 tbsp vegetable oil
  50g/2oz mung bean thread
    noodles, soaked until pliable
  3 hard-boiled eggs, peeled
    and halved
  115g/4oz beansprouts
  a small bunch of fresh coriander
    (cilantro), roughly chopped,
    to garnish
  2 limes, quartered, chilli oil
    and soy sauce, to serve
For the rempah
  8 shallots, chopped
  8 garlic cloves, crushed
    and chopped
  6 candlenuts or macadamia
    nuts
  50g/2oz galangal, chopped
  2 lemon grass stalks, chopped
  4 fresh kaffir lime leaves
  15ml/1 tbsp ground coriander
  10ml/2 tsp ground turmeric
  15ml/1 tbsp vegetable oil

COOK'S TIP
Use a free-range chicken to produce really well-flavoured stock.

1 Using a mortar and pestle or a food processor, grind all the rempah ingredients to a paste. Set aside.

2 Put the chicken, lemon grass, ginger, lime leaves and chilli in a deep pan and pour in enough water to just cover. Bring to the boil, reduce the heat, cover and simmer for about 1 hour, until the chicken is tender.

3 Remove the chicken from the stock, take off and discard the skin and pull the meat from the bones and shred the meat. Strain the stock and reserve.

4 In a wok or heavy pan, heat the oil. Stir in the rempah and cook for 1–2 minutes, until fragrant. Pour in the stock and stir well. Season to taste with salt and pepper.

5 Divide the noodles among six bowls. Add the hard-boiled eggs, beansprouts and shredded chicken. Ladle the steaming broth into each bowl and garnish with coriander.

6 Serve the soup immediately with the lime wedges, chilli oil and soy sauce to squeeze, drizzle and pour over it.

Per Portion Energy 493Kcal/2050kJ; Protein 36g; Carbohydrate 8.5g, of which sugars 1g; Fat 35.1g, of which saturates 9.1g; Cholesterol 258mg; Calcium 47mg; Fibre 0.8g; Sodium 178mg.

PORK BONE TEA

THE LITERAL TRANSLATION OF BAK KUT TEH, PORK BONE TEA, DOESN'T DO JUSTICE TO THIS AROMATIC, PEPPERY BROTH MADE FROM PORK RIBS AND SOMETIMES THE INTERNAL ORGANS OF THE PIG. IT IS A FAVOURITE AT THE LATE-NIGHT HAWKER STALLS AND IN THE COFFEE SHOPS, WHERE IT IS PARTICULARLY POPULAR WITH THE OLDER FOLK, WHO LIKE TO SIP IT WHEN THEY GATHER FOR A CHAT. THE BROTH IS SERVED WITH BOWLS OF STEAMED WHITE RICE, AND THE PIECES OF TENDER PORK FLESH ARE DIPPED INTO SOY SAUCE INFUSED WITH CHILLIES.

1 To make the dipping sauce, stir the soy sauce and chillies together in a small bowl and set aside.

2 To make the spice bag, lay the piece of muslin flat and place all the spices in the centre. Gather up the edges and tie together to form a bag.

3 Put the pork ribs and loin into a deep pan. Add the garlic, cinnamon sticks, star anise and the spice bag. Pour in 2.5 litres/4½ pints/10 cups water and bring to the boil.

4 Skim off any fat from the surface, then stir in the soy sauces and sugar. Reduce the heat and simmer, partially covered, for about 2 hours, until the pork is almost falling off the bones. Season to taste with salt and lots of black pepper.

5 Remove the loin from the broth and cut it into bitesize pieces. Remove the spice bag and discard. Divide the meat and ribs among four to six bowls and ladle the broth over the meat. Remove the star anise and cinnamon, or retain them for decoration only.

6 Serve with the soy and chilli sauce as a dip for the pieces of pork, and steamed rice. Guests will need a fork or chopsticks to eat and dip the pieces of meat and a spoon for the broth.

SERVES FOUR TO SIX

INGREDIENTS
500g/1¼lb meaty pork ribs, trimmed and cut into 5cm/2in lengths
225g/8oz pork loin
8 garlic cloves, unpeeled and bruised
2 cinnamon sticks
5 star anise
120ml/4fl oz/½ cup light soy sauce
50ml/2fl oz/¼ cup dark soy sauce
15ml/1 tbsp sugar

salt and ground black pepper
steamed rice, to serve
For the dipping sauce
120ml/4fl oz/½ cup light soy sauce
2 red chillies, seeded and finely chopped
For the spice bag
6 cloves
15ml/1 tbsp dried orange peel
5ml/1 tsp black peppercorns
5ml/1 tsp coriander seeds
5ml/1 tsp fennel seeds
a piece of muslin (cheesecloth)

Per Portion Energy 49Kcal/206kJ; Protein 8.1g; Carbohydrate 0.8g, of which sugars 0.8g; Fat 1.5g, of which saturates 0.5g; Cholesterol 24mg; Calcium 3mg; Fibre 0g; Sodium 145mg.

BEEF BALL SOUP

THE MAKING OF BEEF BALLS WAS ORIGINALLY A VIETNAMESE WAY OF USING UP CHEAPER CUTS BUT THIS DISH HAS TRANSCENDED RACIAL GROUPS, AS MANY SOUTH VIETNAMESE WERE OF CANTONESE AND TEOCHEW ORIGIN. BEEF BALL SOUP IS NOW SERVED IN MANY CHINESE RESTAURANTS THROUGHOUT SINGAPORE. READY-MADE BEEF BALLS ARE WIDELY AVAILABLE IN CHINESE AND THAI SUPERMARKETS, BUT THEY ARE EASY TO MAKE YOURSELF. USE A LEAN CUT OF BEEF SUCH AS SIRLOIN AND MAKE SURE IT IS FINELY GROUND FOR AN AUTHENTIC TEXTURE.

SERVES FOUR TO SIX

INGREDIENTS
  500g/1¼lb lean minced
    (ground) beef
  15ml/1 tbsp cornflour (cornstarch)
  1 litre/1¾ pints/4 cups water
  5ml/1 tsp salt
  45ml/3 tbsp fish sauce
  1 beef stock cube
  2 cinnamon sticks, each about
    10cm/4 in long
  6 cloves
  2 star anise
  1 large onion, sliced
  6 garlic cloves
  115g/4oz celery stalks
  fresh celery leaves, to garnish
  freshly ground black pepper

1 Put the beef with the cornflour into a pestle and mortar or a food processor, and grind it until very smooth. Add salt and a little water as you go along.

2 Shape the beef into individual balls, each the size of a small lime. To do this, place a small amount in the palm of your hand, form a tight circle with the thumb and fore finger and squeeze. You will get nicely shaped balls.

COOK'S TIP
The longer you process the beef the more springy the resulting texture will be – a requisite for good beef balls.

3 Bring the water to the boil and add the salt, fish sauce, stock cube, cinnamon, cloves, star anise, sliced onion, garlic cloves and celery. Simmer for 30 minutes then strain the stock.

4 Return the stock to the pan and bring to the boil. Drop in the beef balls and cook for 10 minutes. Serve in individual bowls, garnished with celery leaves and ground black pepper.

Per portion Energy 201kcal/837KJ; Protein 16.7g; Carbohydrate 3.3g, of which sugars 0.7g; Fat 13.6g, of which saturates 5.8g; Cholesterol 50mg; Calcium 19mg; Fibre 0.4g; Sodium 456mg.

STREET FOOD AND SNACKS

The appetizing snacks in this chapter are staples of the vibrant street food scene in Singapore. Often eaten hot and fresh from the grill (broiler), they are ideal finger food — there are savoury pancakes and toasts, neat little parcels securely wrapped in pastry, succulent bitesize morsels of fish cooked in crisp batter, and tender pieces of meat such as the classic chicken satay, threaded on sticks and all ready to dip into a delicious spicy sauce.

FRIED INDIAN BREAD

ROTI STALLS ARE GENERALLY RUN BY INDIANS, WHO EXPERTLY KNEAD AND SLAP THE BREAD DOUGHS AND FLICK THEM IN THE AIR BEFORE FRYING THEM ON A GRIDDLE. THIS RECIPE IS FOR THE PLAIN, FLAKY FLATBREAD CALLED ROTI PARATHA. IT IS SERVED WITH CURRIES FOR BREAKFAST, LUNCH AND SUPPER, OR IS SIMPLY SPRINKLED WITH SUGAR FOR A QUICK, SWEET, MID-MORNING SNACK.

SERVES FOUR (MAKES 8 *PARATHAS*)

INGREDIENTS
    225g/8oz/2 cups plain (all-purpose)
    white flour or rice flour
    225g/8oz/2 cups wholemeal
    (whole-wheat) flour
    5ml/1 tsp salt
    200g/7oz/scant 1 cup ghee or butter
    extra flour, for dusting

1 Sift the flours with the salt into a wide bowl. Make a well in the centre and pour in 300ml/½ pint/1¼ cups water. Incorporate the flour gradually, drawing it in from the sides, to make a soft dough. Knead the dough for about 10 minutes, then cover the bowl with a damp dish towel and set aside for 3 hours. Put the ghee or butter into a small pan and melt it over a low heat.

2 Knead the dough again and divide it into 8 portions, rolling each one into a ball – if the dough is sticky, add a little extra flour. Dust a work surface with flour and, using the palm of your hand, flatten one of the balls of dough on it. Roll the dough into an 18cm/7in circle and brush it with the melted ghee.

3 Dust a little flour over the ghee, then roll the paratha into a tight sausage. Wrap it around itself into a coil and place it on the floured surface.

4 Press down on the coil with the palm of your hand to form a patty and roll it into an 18cm/7in circle again. Repeat with the other balls of dough and keep them moist under a damp dish towel.

5 Heat a cast-iron griddle or heavy frying pan and place one paratha on it. Leave it for 30 seconds, then lift it up and brush some ghee under it. Press down on the paratha, moving it around occasionally, for about 2 minutes, then brush some ghee over the top side and flip it over. Cook the second side for about 3 minutes, pressing down on it and moving it around occasionally – it should be nicely browned in patches.

6 Wrap the cooked paratha in foil or a dry dish towel, and repeat with the other balls of dough. They can be cooked and stacked in foil, then heated in the oven before serving. Serve with Indian and Malay curries and soups, or on their own with sugar or jam.

Per Portion Energy 738Kcal/3087kJ; Protein 12.7g; Carbohydrate 80g, of which sugars 2.3g; Fat 43.1g, of which saturates 26.3g; Cholesterol 107mg; Calcium 109mg; Fibre 6.8g; Sodium 798mg.

ONION PANCAKES

A CHINESE DIM SUM STAPLE, THESE PANCAKES ARE NOW ACTUALLY MADE WITH SPRING ONIONS ALTHOUGH THE NAME IS UNCHANGED. YOU CAN USE ONIONS, BUT YOU WON'T GET THE SAME DELICATE FLAVOUR. THIS RECIPE MAKES ABOUT 12 PANCAKES. IT IS ESSENTIAL TO USE LARD TO BRUSH THEM AS OIL WILL NOT GIVE THE SAME FRAGRANCE AND SMOOTH TEXTURE.

SERVES FOUR

INGREDIENTS
   225g/8oz plain (all-purpose) flour
   150ml/¼ pint/⅔ cup water
   15ml/1 tbsp lard
   6 spring onions (scallions), trimmed
    and finely chopped
   5ml/1 tsp salt
   10ml/2 tsp sesame oil
   oil for frying

1 Sift the flour into a large bowl and pour in the water, a little at a time, stirring to create a smooth dough.

2 Work the dough until it is soft and pliable. Knead for 5 minutes and set aside, covered with a damp cloth, for 20 minutes.

3 Divide the dough into 12 pieces. Roll out into rectangles 5mm/¼in thick.

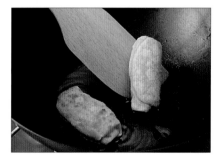

4 Toss the spring onions with salt and sesame oil. Brush each pancake with melted lard and scatter with some of the chopped spring onions.

5 Roll up the pancakes lengthways to encase the onions then flatten slightly so that they will not unwrap during cooking.

COOK'S TIP
Eat the pancakes just as they are or with soy sauce or another dipping sauce.

6 Heat a wok with about 15ml/1 tbsp oil and fry the pancakes one or two at a time until light brown along the edges. Add more oil as required.

7 Flip over and cook the other side. Each pancake should take about 3 minutes to cook and puff up slightly.

Per portion Energy 242Kcal/1023kJ; Protein 5.6g; Carbohydrate 44.2g, of which sugars 1.3g; Fat 6g, of which saturates 1.9g; Cholesterol 3mg; Calcium 85mg; Fibre 2g; Sodium 494mg.

SAMOSAS

THESE TASTY VEGETARIAN PARCELS TRAVELLED TO SINGAPORE WITH MIGRANT INDIAN WORKERS IN THE 19TH CENTURY. THEY ARE AN IDEAL STREET SNACK, EATEN AT ANY TIME OF DAY. FILO PASTRY CAN BE USED INSTEAD OF SPRING ROLL WRAPPERS IF YOU PREFER.

MAKES ABOUT 20

INGREDIENTS
1 packet 25cm/10in square spring roll wrappers, thawed if frozen
30ml/2 tbsp plain (all-purpose) flour, mixed to a paste with water
vegetable oil, for deep frying
coriander (cilantro) leaves, to garnish
cucumber, carrot and celery, cut into matchsticks, to serve (optional)
For the filling
25g/1oz/2 tbsp ghee or unsalted butter
1 small onion, finely chopped
1cm/½in piece fresh root ginger, peeled and chopped
1 garlic clove, crushed
2.5ml/½ tsp chilli powder
1 large potato, about 225g/8oz, cooked until just tender and finely diced
50g/2oz/½ cup cauliflower florets, lightly cooked, chopped into small pieces
50g/2oz/½ cup frozen peas, thawed
5–10ml/1–2 tsp garam masala
15ml/1 tbsp chopped fresh coriander (leaves and stems)
squeeze of lemon juice
salt

1 Heat the ghee or butter in a large wok and fry the onion, ginger and garlic for 5 minutes until the onion has softened. Add the chilli powder, cook for 1 minute, then stir in the cauliflower, potato and peas. Sprinkle with garam masala and set aside to cool. Stir in the coriander, lemon juice and salt.

2 Cut the spring roll wrappers into three strips (or two for larger samosas). Brush the edges with a little of the flour paste. Place a small spoonful of filling about 2cm/¾in in from the edge of one strip.

3 Fold one corner over the filling to make a triangle and continue this folding until the entire strip has been used and a triangular pastry packet has been formed.

4 Seal any open edges with more flour and water paste, if necessary adding more water if the paste is very thick.

5 In a wok or heavy pan heat the oil to 190°C/375°F and deep fry the samosas, a few at a time, until golden and crisp. Drain well on kitchen paper and serve hot garnished with coriander leaves and accompanied by crunchy cucumber, carrot and celery matchsticks, if liked.

Per portion Energy 56Kcal/2351kJ; Protein 1.4g; Carbohydrate 10.4g, of which sugars 0.6g; Fat 1.3g, of which saturates 0.7g; Cholesterol 3mg; Calcium 17mg; Fibre 0.6g; Sodium 9mg.

OYSTER OMELETTE

OFTEN DEVOURED AS A LATE-NIGHT TREAT, OYSTER OMELETTE IS A FAVOURITE HAWKER STALL SNACK IN SINGAPORE. ALMOST DECADENT IN ITS LAVISH USE OF OYSTERS, THIS IS A TASTY AND SATISFYING DISH, THAT WAS ORIGINALLY INSPIRED BY THE CHINESE.

SERVES TWO

INGREDIENTS
    30ml/2 tbsp vegetable oil
    2 garlic cloves, finely chopped
    1 red chilli, finely chopped
    8 large fresh oysters, shelled
        and rinsed
    15ml/1 tbsp light soy sauce
    15ml/1 tbsp Chinese wine
    4 eggs, lightly beaten with
        30ml/2 tbsp milk
    8 small fresh oysters, shelled
        and rinsed
    chilli oil
    salt and ground black pepper
    fresh coriander (cilantro) leaves,
        finely chopped, to garnish

COOK'S TIP
In Penang a generous splash of oyster sauce is added with the small oysters.

1 Heat the oil in a heavy frying pan. Stir in the garlic and chilli until they become fragrant. Add the large oysters and cook for 1 minute, then stir in the soy sauce and Chinese wine. Season with salt and black pepper.

2 Pour in the beaten egg mixture and, using a wooden spatula, pull it back from the edge of the pan until it begins to solidify.

3 Reduce the heat. Scatter the small oysters over the top of the egg and drizzle with chilli oil. Cover the pan and leave to steam for 5–10 minutes until firm. Sprinkle the omelette with chopped coriander, cut it into wedges and serve it from the pan.

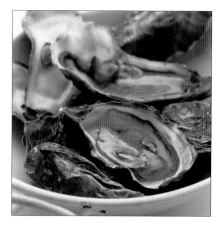

Per Portion Energy 370Kcal/1543kJ; Protein 32.2g; Carbohydrate 6.1g, of which sugars 1.3g; Fat 24.6g, of which saturates 4.9g; Cholesterol 481mg; Calcium 322mg; Fibre 0g; Sodium 1573mg.

CRAB TOFU PARCELS

THIS IS AN INNOVATIVE WAY TO USE CRAB MEAT AND IS A STAPLE DISH IN CHINESE RESTAURANTS. USE ONLY THE FRESHEST CRAB MEAT OR TOP-QUALITY CANNED CRAB MEAT. MOST LONG-LIFE TOFU COMES IN TWO TYPES, SOFT AND FIRM. USE THE FIRM VARIETY FOR THESE PARCELS.

SERVES FOUR

INGREDIENTS
    150g/5oz fresh or canned
        crab meat
    5ml/1 tsp cornflour (cornstarch)
    1 egg, lightly beaten
    15 ml/1 tbsp sesame oil
    2 packets firm tofu, about
        500g/1¼lb
    2 spring onions (scallions), trimmed
        and finely chopped
    salt and ground black pepper

1 Lightly crush the crab meat and mix to a paste with the cornflour and beaten egg.

2 Add salt, pepper and sesame oil and mix thoroughly.

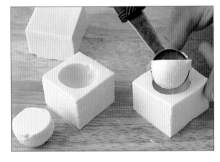

3 Divide the tofu into 4 square pieces. With a melon baller, gently scoop out a hollow in each piece.

4 Fill each hollow with the crab meat mixture and place in a deep plate. Sprinkle each piece with finely chopped spring onion.

5 Steam the parcels for 5 minutes and serve as a warm appetizer.

Per portion Energy 170Kcal/706kJ; Protein 18.6g; Carbohydrate 2g, of which sugars 0.5g; Fat 9.8g, of which saturates 1.5g; Cholesterol 75mg; Calcium 692mg; Fibre 0.1g; Sodium 230mg.

SWEET AND SOUR DEEP-FRIED SQUID

DEEP-FRIED SQUID SERVED WITH A SWEET AND SOUR SAUCE IS POPULAR WITH MALAYS, CHINESE AND EURASIANS. THIS IS AN EXAMPLE OF A DISH WHERE THE WESTERN INFLUENCE COMES INTO PLAY – THE DIPPING SAUCE IS MADE USING TOMATO KETCHUP AND WORCESTERSHIRE SAUCE.

SERVES FOUR

INGREDIENTS
    900g/2lb fresh young, tender squid
    vegetable oil, for deep-frying
For the marinade
    60ml/4 tbsp light soy sauce
    15ml/1 tbsp sugar
For the dipping sauce
    30ml/2 tbsp tomato ketchup
    15ml/1 tbsp Worcestershire sauce
    15ml/1 tbsp light soy sauce
    15ml/1 tbsp vegetable or sesame oil
    sugar or honey, to sweeten
    chilli oil, to taste

COOK'S TIP
To avoid the spitting fat, lightly coat the squid in flour before deep-frying. Alternatively, fry in a deep-fat fryer with a lid or use a spatterproof cover on the wok or pan.

1 First prepare the squid. Hold the body in one hand and pull off the head with the other. Sever the tentacles and discard the rest. Remove the backbone and clean the body sac inside and out. Pat dry using kitchen paper and cut into rings.

2 In a bowl, mix the soy sauce with the sugar until it dissolves. Toss in the squid rings and tentacles and leave to marinate for 1 hour.

3 Meanwhile prepare the sauce. Mix together the tomato ketchup, soy sauce, Worcestershire sauce and oil. Sweeten with sugar or honey to taste and add as much chilli oil as you like. Set aside until ready to serve.

4 Heat enough oil for deep-frying in a wok or heavy pan. Thoroughly drain the squid of any marinade, pat well with kitchen paper to avoid spitting, and fry the squid rings until they are golden and crispy. Drain on kitchen paper and serve immediately, accompanied by the dipping sauce.

Per Portion Energy 315Kcal/1320kJ; Protein 35.2g; Carbohydrate 4.5g, of which sugars 1.7g; Fat 17.6g, of which saturates 2.5g; Cholesterol 506mg; Calcium 39mg; Fibre 0g; Sodium 1361mg.

MINCED PORK AND TARO PUFFS

A DIM SUM FAVOURITE, THESE ARE CALLED WU KOK IN CANTONESE AND THEY MAKE VERY SAVOURY SNACKS. TARO, OTHERWISE KNOWN AS YAM, IS SOLD IN MOST CHINESE SUPERMARKETS.

3 Mix the pork with the cornflour and moisten the mixture with a little water. Heat the vegetable oil in a pan and fry the pork until nearly cooked. Stir in all other filling ingredients.

4 Remove from the heat and leave to cool a little. Meanwhile, divide the dough into four portions and roll out into flat rounds.

5 Fill each round with 15ml/1 tbsp of the pork mixture. Shape into an oval pasty, sealing the pastry well around the filling. Dust with cornflour and deep-fry until golden brown.

SERVES FOUR

INGREDIENTS
　cornflour (cornstarch), for dusting
　oil, for deep-frying
For the pastry
　500g/1¼lb taro
　30ml/2 tbsp plain (all-purpose) flour
　15ml/1 tbsp lard
　pinch of bicarbonate of soda
　　(baking soda)
　15ml/1 tbsp sesame oil
　5ml/1 tsp sugar
　salt and ground black pepper
For the filling
　150g/5oz minced (ground) pork
　5ml/1 tsp cornflour (cornstarch)
　30ml/2 tbsp vegetable oil
　30ml/2 tbsp frozen peas
　5g/1 tsp sugar
　15ml/1 tbsp sesame oil
　salt and ground black pepper

1 To make the pastry, peel the taro and cut it into chunks. Steam for about 15 minutes until soft. Mash while still warm and mix with the remaining pastry ingredients to form a dough.

2 Turn out on to a lightly floured board and knead until the dough is soft and pliable. Set it aside while you make the filling, covered with a damp dish towel to prevent it drying out.

Per portion Energy 367Kcal/1541kJ; Protein 11.2g; Carbohydrate 45.7g, of which sugars 3.8g; Fat 16.8g, of which saturates 3.7g; Cholesterol 27mg; Calcium 36mg; Fibre 2.2g; Sodium 30mg.

POPIAH

THIS IS A GREAT DO-IT-YOURSELF DISH. IT IS SIMILAR TO THE VIETNAMESE RICE PAPER ROLL, WHERE THE WRAPS AND INGREDIENTS ARE PREPARED AND SELF-ASSEMBLED AT THE DINNER TABLE.

SERVES FOUR TO SIX

INGREDIENTS

45ml/3 tbsp vegetable oil
225g/8oz firm tofu, rinsed,
    drained and diced
4 garlic cloves, finely chopped
4 rashers (strips) streaky (fatty)
    bacon, finely sliced
45ml/3 tbsp fermented soya
    beans (tau cheo), mashed to
    a paste
450g/1lb fresh prawns (shrimp),
    peeled and deveined
225g/8oz jicama (sweet turnip),
    peeled and shredded
450g/1lb bamboo shoots, rinsed
    and grated
15ml/1 tbsp dark soy sauce
10ml/2 tsp sugar
4–6 red chillies, seeded and
    pounded to a paste
6–8 garlic cloves, pounded to
    a paste
kecap manis, to serve
12 cos or romaine lettuce leaves,
    washed and patted dry
1 small cucumber, peeled, seeded
    and finely shredded
225g/8oz beansprouts, washed
    and drained
2 Chinese sausages, fried
    and sliced
225g/8oz cooked prawns (shrimp),
    peeled
225g/8oz cooked crab meat
3 eggs, beaten and fried to form
    a plain omelette, sliced into
    thin ribbons
fresh coriander (cilantro) leaves,
    roughly chopped
12 popiah wraps or Mexican
    corn tortillas

1 Heat the oil in a wok or heavy pan. Fry the tofu until golden. Remove from the oil and pat dry on kitchen paper.

2 Fry the garlic and bacon in the oil, stirring constantly, until they begin to colour. Stir in the fermented soya beans and fresh prawns.

3 Add the jicama, bamboo shoots, soy sauce and sugar. Fry over a high heat to reduce the water released from the jicama. Toss in the fried tofu and cook the mixture gently until almost dry. Transfer to a serving dish.

4 Assemble the remaining ingredients in separate bowls and place them on the table. Place the wraps on a plate.

5 To serve, everyone should help themselves to a wrap and smear it with the chilli and garlic pastes, followed by the kecap manis. A lettuce leaf goes on top followed by cucumber, beansprouts, and the cooked filling. Add Chinese sausage, prawns and crab, a few strips of omelette and a little coriander, then roll up the wrap, tucking in the ends, to make a tight package.

Per Portion Energy 457Kcal/1916kJ; Protein 32.3g; Carbohydrate 39.2g, of which sugars 5.8g; Fat 20.1g, of which saturates 4.9g; Cholesterol 213mg; Calcium 396mg; Fibre 4.5g; Sodium 989mg.

CHICKEN SATAY

THIS POPULAR DISH IS A DELICACY THAT EVERY SOUTH-EAST ASIAN COUNTRY CLAIMS AS THEIR OWN. HOWEVER, SINGAPORE CAN BOAST SOME OF THE BEST AVAILABLE, AND ITS MANY SATAY STALLS ALONG BEACH ROAD IN THE 1950s CAME TO BE KNOWN AS THE SATAY CLUB.

MAKES ABOUT 20–24 STICKS

INGREDIENTS
  500g/1¼lb chicken breast, cut into
    pieces 4 x 2.5 x 1cm/1½ x 1 x ½in
  20–24 bamboo or wooden skewers,
    soaked in water
For the marinade
  15ml/1 tbsp ground coriander
  15ml/1 tbsp ground cumin
  5ml/1 tsp ground turmeric
  5ml/1 tsp chilli powder
  150ml/5 fl oz/¾ cup coconut milk
  5ml/1 tsp salt
  10ml/2 tsp sugar
  45ml/3 tbsp oil
  1 stalk lemon grass, bruised at
    the root end to make a brush
For the sauce (makes about 1 litre/
1¾ pints/4 cups)
  2 large onions, roughly chopped

  4 cloves garlic, roughly chopped
  25g/1oz shrimp paste
  15g/½oz galangal, roughly chopped
  2 stalks lemon grass, 7.5cm/3in of
    root end
  10 dried chillies, soaked until soft
    and seeds removed (optional for
    milder flavour)
  300g/11oz peanuts, finely ground
  45ml/3 tbsp tamarind concentrate
  400ml/14 fl oz/1⅔ cups water
  10ml/2 tsp salt
  25g/1oz sugar
  150ml/5 fl oz/⅔ cup vegetable oil

COOK'S TIP
Add the ground peanuts to the sauce just before serving the satay, otherwise they tend to settle down and make the sauce too stiff. If this happens, warm it in a microwave oven for 1–2 minutes.

1 Blend together all the ingredients for the marinade in a large non-metallic bowl or dish. Add the chicken breast pieces and marinate for several hours or leave overnight.

2 To make the sauce, grind the onions, garlic, shrimp paste, galangal, lemon grass and chillies to make a fine paste. Heat the oil and fry the paste over medium heat for 15 minutes, stirring constantly. When the oil separates, add the tamarind blended with the water and bring to the boil. Season to taste with salt and sugar and simmer for 10 minutes.

3 Thread 3–4 pieces of chicken on to each stick, pressing them together. Grill (broil) over hot coals or under a hot grill (broiler) for 8 minutes, turning once.

4 Dip the lemon grass in oil and baste them to impart a delicious lemony tang.

5 Heat the sauce through, add the ground nuts and stir well. Remove from the heat immediately and serve with the satay sticks.

Per portion Energy 33Kcal/139kJ; Protein 7.1g; Carbohydrate 0.4g, of which sugars 0.3g; Fat 0.3g, of which saturates 0.1g; Cholesterol 20mg; Calcium 2mg; Fibre 0.1g; Sodium 107mg.

CHARGRILLED SPICY CHICKEN WINGS

SPICY GRILLED CHICKEN JOINTS ARE VERY POPULAR AS A QUICK SNACK, WHICH CAN EVEN BE ENJOYED ON THE MOVE. THEY ARE OFTEN SERVED ON THEIR OWN, OR FORM PART OF THE SELECTION OF DISHES ON DISPLAY AT THE TZE CHAR STALLS, WHERE PEOPLE FILL THEIR BOWLS WITH WHATEVER THEY WANT.

SERVES FOUR

INGREDIENTS
  12 chicken wings
  fresh coriander (cilantro) leaves,
    roughly chopped, and 2–3 green
    chillies, seeded and quartered
    lengthways, to garnish
For the spice paste
  4 shallots, chopped
  4 garlic cloves, chopped
  25g/1oz fresh root ginger, chopped
  8 red chillies, seeded and chopped
  1 lemon grass stalk, trimmed
    and chopped
  30ml/2 tbsp sesame or groundnut
    (peanut) oil
  15ml/1 tbsp tomato purée (paste)
  10ml/2 tsp sugar
  juice of 2 limes
  salt and ground black pepper

VARIATION
If you prefer boneless chicken, use 6 halved breast fillets instead of the wings and cook them in the same way.

1 First make the spice paste. Using a mortar and pestle or food processor, grind the shallots, garlic, ginger, chillies and lemon grass to a paste. Bind with the oil and stir in the tomato purée, sugar and lime juice. Season with salt and pepper.

2 Rub the spice paste into the chicken wings and leave to marinate for 2 hours.

3 Prepare the charcoal grill. Lift the chicken wings out of the marinade and place them on the rack. Cook them for about 5 minutes each side until cooked through, brushing with the remaining marinade while they cook.

4 Serve the chicken wings immediately, garnished with chopped coriander and slivers of chilli.

Per Portion Energy 350Kcal/1455kJ; Protein 30.7g; Carbohydrate 2.6g, of which sugars 2.6g; Fat 24.1g, of which saturates 5.9g; Cholesterol 134mg; Calcium 11mg; Fibre 0.1g; Sodium 99mg.

RICE AND NOODLES

Either rice or noodles are eaten with every meal in Singapore,

from breakfast to late-night snacks; many noodles are

themselves made of rice. A bowl of simple steamed or boiled

rice is filling and nourishing, and provides the background for

vibrantly spiced meat, fish and vegetable accompaniments.

Soft, comforting noodles go into fragrant broths with meat or

fish balls, and are tossed into countless stir-fries to make

satisfying and speedy meals.

COMPRESSED RICE CAKES

THESE COMPRESSED RICE CAKES ARE COOKED IN LITTLE WOVEN PACKAGES MADE FROM STRIPS OF PALM FRONDS AND SERVED WITH SATAY. THE PACKAGES CONTAINING THE UNCOOKED RICE ARE TIED IN BUNDLES AND LOWERED INTO A DEEP PAN OF BOILING WATER, WHERE THEY ARE LEFT TO SIMMER OVER A VERY LOW HEAT FOR ABOUT 3 HOURS. TO MAKE THEM IN A WESTERN HOME, IT'S EASIER TO PRE-COOK THE RICE AND THEN STEAM IT IN FOIL OR BANANA LEAVES.

SERVES FOUR

INGREDIENTS
225g/8oz/generous 1 cup short
    grain rice, thoroughly washed
    and drained
2.5ml/½ tsp salt
dipping sauce, to serve
4 sheets of aluminium foil, each
    measuring 20 x 30cm/8 x 12in

1 In a heavy pan, bring 600ml/1 pint/ 2½ cups water to the boil. Stir in the rice and salt. When the water starts to bubble again, reduce the heat and cover the pan. Allow to simmer for about 20 minutes, until all the water has been absorbed.

2 Spoon one-quarter of the rice about 2.5cm/1in in from the shorter edge of each foil sheet, then roll up loosely, leaving room for the rice to expand. Twist the ends to seal. Place the parcels in a bamboo steamer set in a wok, or a conventional steamer.

3 Steam for 40 minutes, then leave the parcels to cool, twisting the ends more tightly if necessary, before unwrapping. Slice the compressed rice into bitesize rounds and serve with a Malay curry dish, satay or simply with soy sauce or a sambal for dipping.

Per Portion Energy 202Kcal/845kJ; Protein 4.2g; Carbohydrate 44.9g, of which sugars 0g; Fat 0.3g, of which saturates 0g; Cholesterol 0mg; Calcium 11mg; Fibre 0g; Sodium 164mg.

PANDAN LEAF RICE

ALMOST EVERY KITCHEN GARDEN IN SOUTH-EAST ASIA HAS A PANDAN OR SCREWPINE PLANT, AND THE LONG LEAVES ARE USED TO PERFUME BOTH SWEET AND SAVOURY DISHES. THIS RICE DISH IS NOTABLE FOR ITS SUBTLE PERFUME. IT IS SOMETIMES MADE WITH GLUTINOUS RICE AND TOPPED WITH STRIPS OF OMELETTE. BECAUSE THE RICE IS STEAMED, LESS WATER IS REQUIRED THAN WHEN COOKING BY THE ABSORPTION METHOD. THE LONG SOAKING ALSO HELPS TO SHORTEN THE STEAMING TIME.

SERVES FOUR

INGREDIENTS
  250g/9oz/1¼ cups glutinous rice
  10g/2 tsp salt
  4 pandan (screwpine) leaves,
    cut into 10cm/4in lengths

1 Wash the glutinous rice and put it in a large bowl or dish with cold water to cover the rice. Leave to soak for at least 2 hours, then drain the water.

2 Line a steaming tray with a muslin (cheesecloth) and place the soaked rice in the tray and add 400ml/14fl oz/ 1⅔ cups water. Add the salt, stirring it into the rice to distribute well.

3 Arrange the lengths of pandan leaves all over the rice, pressing a few into the surface.

4 Steam for 20 minutes, until the rice grains are soft and tender. Discard the pandan leaves and serve the cooked rice with curries and sambals.

Per portion Energy 238Kcal/995kJ; Protein 6g; Carbohydrate 49.3g, of which sugars 2.5g; Fat 1.1g, of which saturates 0g; Cholesterol 0mg; Calcium 35mg; Fibre 1.1g; Sodium 988mg.

SINGAPORE VEGETARIAN BEE HOON

DURING BUDDHIST FESTIVALS THIS DISH IS SERVED AT MOST TEMPLES. THE CLASSIC INGREDIENTS ARE RICE VERMICELLI (BEE HOON), SLICED CABBAGE, FRIED BEAN CURD WAFERS AND MUSHROOMS. THESE CAN BE BULKED UP WITH BEANSPROUTS AND SLICED FRENCH BEANS.

SERVES FOUR

INGREDIENTS
    oil for deep-frying
    6 bean curd wafers
    4 garlic cloves, crushed
    100g/3½oz thinly sliced cabbage
    10 canned Chinese black
       mushrooms, thinly sliced
    100g/3½oz beansprouts
    200ml/7 fl oz/scant 1 cup water
    175g/6oz bee hoon, soaked
       until soft
    30ml/2 tbsp light soy sauce
    freshly ground black pepper

COOK'S TIP
If you are using dried Chinese mushrooms, soak them in warm water for 30 minutes before slicing.

1 Heat the oil in a wok and fry the bean curd wafers until they are crisp. Remove and drain on kitchen paper.

2 Put 30ml/2 tbsp fresh oil in the wok and fry the garlic until golden brown. Add the cabbage, mushrooms and beansprouts and stir-fry for 5 minutes. Add the water and stir for 1 minute.

3 Add the bee hoon and continue to stir until it is heated through and well blended with the other ingredients. Add the light soy sauce and season to taste with black pepper.

4 Cut the fried bean curd wafers into strips and use them to garnish the fried bee hoon. Serve immediately.

Per portion Energy 330Kcal/1377kJ; Protein 17.5g; Carbohydrate 49.9g, of which sugars 4.5g; Fat 6.6g, of which saturates 0.8g; Cholesterol 110mg; Calcium 125mg; Fibre 1.9g; Sodium 960mg.

PERAK SOUR LAKSA

A LAKSA IS ANY SPICY NOODLE DISH, OF WHICH THERE ARE MANY DIFFERENT KINDS. SINGAPORE LAKSA IS RICH IN COCONUT MILK. IN SINGAPORE THERE ARE STREETS WHERE THREE, FOUR OR MORE STALLS SELL LAKSA, EACH CLAIMING TO HAVE BEEN THE ORIGINATOR.

SERVES TWO TO THREE

INGREDIENTS
    45ml/3 tbsp oil
    2 whole mackerel, gutted and
        cleaned
    1 large onion, sliced
    45ml/3 tbsp lime juice
    5ml/1 tsp salt
    5ml/1 tsp sugar
    ½ cucumber
    200g/7oz bee hoon (rice vermicelli),
        soaked until soft
    6–8 laksa leaves
For the spice paste
    5 red chillies
    6 shallots
    15g/½oz shrimp paste
    15g/½oz fresh turmeric
    3 garlic cloves
    1 stalk lemon grass, trimmed to
        7.5cm/3in at the root end

1 To make the spice paste, grind all the ingredients using a mortar and pestle and pound to a smooth paste. Alternatively, put all the ingredients into a blender or food processor and blend to a smooth paste.

2 Heat the oil in a wok or large frying pan and fry the spice paste for about 3 minutes until fragrant. Set aside.

3 Put the cleaned mackerel and the sliced onion in a pan with 600ml/ 1 pint/2½ cups water. Bring to the boil and simmer for 10 minutes. Remove the mackerel, debone and flake the flesh. Set aside.

4 Continue to simmer the stock for about 15 minutes, or until the onion is completely soft. Strain the stock and discard the onion. Add the stock to the wok and stir it into the fried spice paste. Simmer for 5 minutes.

5 Add the lime juice, salt and sugar to the stock, adjusting the seasoning to taste. Return the flaked mackerel to the wok and bring to a gentle simmer. Cook for 3 minutes, then remove from the heat and keep warm.

6 Peel and de-seed the cucumber and shred very finely. To serve, divide the bee hoon into two or three portions and top with some of the mackerel. Ladle the stock over the top and garnish with laksa leaves and cucumber.

COOK'S TIP
Have extra lime juice to hand to add to the stock at the last minute if you prefer the laksa to be quite sour. The tangy flavour goes well with the mellow richness of the fish.

Per portion Energy 593Kcal/2468kJ; Protein 28.3g; Carbohydrate 56.8g, of which sugars 3g; Fat 28g, of which saturates 4.7g; Cholesterol 79mg; Calcium 104mg; Fibre 0.5g; Sodium 943mg.

Chinese Clay Pot Rice with Chicken

This Cantonese dish is a great family one-pot meal. It can also be found on Chinese stalls and in some coffee shops. The traditional clay pot ensures that the ingredients remain moist, while allowing the flavours to mingle.

SERVES FOUR

INGREDIENTS

500g/1¼ lb chicken breast fillets,
  cut into thin strips
5 dried Chinese (shiitake)
  mushrooms, soaked in hot water for
  30 minutes, until soft
1 Chinese sausage, sliced
750ml/1¼pints/3 cups chicken stock
225g/8oz/generous 1 cup long grain
  rice, thoroughly washed and drained
fresh coriander (cilantro) leaves,
  finely chopped, to garnish
For the marinade
30ml/2 tbsp sesame oil
45ml/3 tbsp oyster sauce
30ml/2 tbsp soy sauce
25g/1oz fresh root ginger, finely
  grated (shredded)
2 spring onions (scallions), trimmed
  and finely sliced
1 red chilli, seeded and finely sliced
5ml/1 tsp sugar
ground black pepper

1 In a bowl, mix together the ingredients for the marinade. Toss in the chicken, making sure it is well coated. Set aside.

2 Check that the shiitake mushrooms are soft (leave them to soak for longer, if necessary). Squeeze them to get rid of any excess water.

3 Using a sharp knife, remove any hard stems from the mushrooms and cut the caps in half. Add the caps and the Chinese sausage to the chicken.

4 Bring the stock to the boil in the clay pot. Stir in the rice and bring it back to the boil. Reduce the heat, cover the pot, and leave to simmer on a low heat for 15–20 minutes, until almost all the liquid has been absorbed.

5 Spread the marinated mixture over the top of the rice and cover the pot again. Leave to steam for about 10–15 minutes, until all the liquid is absorbed and the chicken is cooked. Garnish the rice with chopped coriander and serve at once.

COOK'S TIP
Remember, if you are using a newly bought clay pot, you need to season it first to stop it cracking. Fill it with water and slowly bring it to the boil. Simmer for 5–10 minutes, then leave it to cool. Pour out the water and wipe the pot dry. Now it is ready to use.

Per Portion Energy 371Kcal/1560kJ; Protein 36.2g; Carbohydrate 46.8g, of which sugars 1g; Fat 4g, of which saturates 1.2g; Cholesterol 93mg; Calcium 54mg; Fibre 0.7g; Sodium 721mg.

LOTUS-LEAF RICE

THIS DISH IS EATEN ON FESTIVE OCCASIONS BUT IS ALSO A TASTY DIM SUM ITEM IN RESTAURANTS. LOTUS SEEDS ARE ADDED FOR FLAVOUR AND TEXTURE AS WELL AS FOR SYMBOLIC REASONS, AS THEY REPRESENT FERTILITY. THE LEAVES ARE AVAILABLE IN ALL CHINESE STORES AND NEED ONLY BE WIPED BEFORE USE. THEY IMPART A DISTINCTIVE FLAVOUR AND MAKE AN IMPRESSIVE DISPLAY WHEN OPENED.

SERVES FOUR

INGREDIENTS
   250g/9oz/1¼ cups sticky (glutinous)
    rice, soaked for at least 2 hours,
    then drained
   250ml/8fl oz/1 cup water
   10ml/2 tsp salt
   2 large lotus leaves
For the filling
   150g/5oz chicken breast
   4 dried Chinese (shiitake)
    mushrooms, soaked until soft, or
    canned mushrooms
   30ml/2 tbsp vegetable oil
   3 garlic cloves, crushed
   30ml/2 tbsp oyster sauce
   5ml/1 tsp ground black pepper
   15ml/1 tbsp sesame oil
   45ml/3 tbsp water
   20 canned lotus seeds

1 Put the soaked rice in a steamer, add the water and salt and steam for 20 minutes. Set aside to cool.

2 To make the filling, slice the chicken into small dice and cut each mushroom into quarters. Heat the vegetable oil and fry the garlic until golden brown. Add the pieces of chicken and stir-fry for 2 minutes.

3 Add the mushrooms, oyster sauce, lotus seeds, pepper, sesame oil and water and continue to stir until the chicken is completely cooked.

4 Spread out the lotus leaves, laying one on top of the other to ensure against splitting or leaking.

5 Spread the steamed rice on top, flattening it with a spatula. Spread the chicken and mushrooms evenly over it.

6 Make a firm parcel with the lotus leaves, tucking the ends under to secure. Steam for 5 minutes or microwave for 2 minutes before serving.

Per portion Energy 377Kcal/1581kJ; Protein 20.7g; Carbohydrate 63.7g, of which sugars 2.4g; Fat 4g, of which saturates 1.2g; Cholesterol 43mg; Calcium 31mg; Fibre 0.8g; Sodium 1082mg.

CANTONESE FRIED RICE

THERE ARE MANY RECIPES FOR FRIED RICE, BUT THE CANTONESE, WHEREVER THEY MAY LIVE, ARE PAST MASTERS AT TRANSFORMING WHAT IS BASICALLY A HUMBLE DISH DEVISED TO USE UP YESTERDAY'S LEFTOVER RICE INTO ONE FIT FOR EMPERORS. IT IS ALSO A VERY ADAPTABLE CREATION, AS YOU CAN ADD EXTRA INGREDIENTS OF YOUR CHOICE, FROM CHICKEN TO KING PRAWNS OR SCALLOPS.

SERVES FOUR

INGREDIENTS
- 600g/1lb 6oz cooked cold rice
- 60ml/4 tbsp oil
- ½ large onion, chopped
- 3 eggs
- 100g/3¾oz lean cooked ham, cubed
- 100g/3¾oz raw, shelled prawns (shrimp)
- 50g/2oz canned crab meat
- 50g/2oz frozen peas
- 2 spring onions (scallions), trimmed and finely sliced
- 30ml/2 tbsp light soy sauce
- ½ tsp sugar
- freshly ground black pepper
- sliced cucumber and chilli sauce, to serve

1 If the rice has been refrigerated, rake it with a fork to loosen the grains.

2 Heat the oil in a wok or heavy pan and fry the onion until soft, but not brown. Push to one side and crack in the eggs. Cook until set, cutting them up roughly with a spatula.

3 Push the eggs to one side and add the ham, prawns and crab meat.

4 Stir-fry for 2 minutes, then add the rice and stir vigorously until heated through. Add the peas, spring onions, soy sauce and sugar and black pepper. Serve with cucumber and chilli sauce.

Per portion Energy 437Kcal/1837kJ; Protein 20.4g; Carbohydrate 51g, of which sugars 2.3g; Fat 18.4g, of which saturates 3.3g; Cholesterol 211mg; Calcium 84mg; Fibre 1.1g; Sodium 1025mg.

SINGAPORE EGG NOODLES

OTHERWISE KNOWN AS HOKKIEN MEE, *THIS IS A VERY POPULAR STIR-FRIED DISH IN* SINGAPORE, *WHERE MOST OF THE* CHINESE *POPULATION IS* HOKKIEN. *IT TAKES ITS NAME FROM THE PEOPLE, AS WELL AS FROM THE THICK NOODLES, CALLED* HOKKIEN *NOODLES.*

SERVES FOUR

INGREDIENTS
    30ml/2 tbsp vegetable oil
    3 garlic cloves, finely chopped
    115g/4oz pork fillet, cut into
        thin strips
    115g/4oz fresh fish fillets
        (such as red snapper, grouper
        or trout), cut into bitesize
        pieces
    115g/4oz fresh prawns (shrimp),
        shelled and deveined
    2 small squid, with innards and
        quill removed, trimmed, cleaned,
        skinned and sliced (reserve
        tentacles)

    300ml/½ pint/1¼ cups
        chicken stock
    450g/1lb fresh egg noodles
    1 carrot, shredded
    6 long white Chinese cabbage
        leaves, shredded
    30ml/2 tbsp dark soy sauce
    30ml/2 tbsp light soy sauce
    ground black pepper
    a small bunch of fresh coriander
        (cilantro), roughly chopped

1 Heat the oil in a wok and stir in the garlic. When it becomes fragrant, stir in the pork, fish, prawns and squid, tossing them around the pan for 1 minute. Pour in the stock and bubble it up to reduce it.

2 Add the noodles and toss them around the wok for 1 minute. Stir in the shredded carrot and cabbage, add the soy sauces and cook until most of the liquid has evaporated. Season with pepper, sprinkle with coriander, divide the noodles among four bowls and eat while steaming hot.

Per Portion Energy 609Kcal/2571kJ; Protein 35.2g; Carbohydrate 84.4g, of which sugars 5.3g; Fat 16.9g, of which saturates 3.8g; Cholesterol 186mg; Calcium 81mg; Fibre 4.2g; Sodium 867mg.

CHINESE STIR-FRIED NOODLES

THIS CHINESE DISH OF STIR-FRIED RICE NOODLES AND SEAFOOD IS ONE OF THE MOST POPULAR AT THE HAWKER STALLS OF SINGAPORE, SERVED AT BREAKFAST, LUNCH, SUPPER, MID-MORNING, MID-AFTERNOON OR LATE EVENING. VARIATIONS INCLUDE RED SNAPPER, CLAMS AND PORK.

SERVES THREE TO FOUR

INGREDIENTS

2 small squid, trimmed, cleaned
   and skinned
12 fresh prawns (shrimp), washed
   and peeled
45ml/3 tbsp vegetable oil
2 garlic cloves, finely chopped
2 red chillies, seeded and finely
   sliced
1 Chinese sausage, finely sliced
500g/1¼lb fresh rice noodles
30ml/2 tbsp light soy sauce
45ml/3 tbsp kecap manis
2–3 mustard greens, chopped
a handful of beansprouts
2 eggs, lightly beaten
ground black pepper
fresh coriander (cilantro) leaves,
   finely chopped, to serve, plus
   a few reserved sprigs for
   decoration

COOK'S TIP
If you are unable to find kecap manis in your local Asian food store, market or supermarket, you can replace it with the same quantity of dark soy sauce mixed with a little sugar.

1 Slice the cleaned squid into strips or rings about 1cm/⅓ in wide. Check that the prawns have all their shells and veins removed, removing any veins with a sharp knife.

2 Heat a wok or large frying pan and add the oil. Stir in the garlic and chillies and fry until fragrant.

3 Add the Chinese sausage, then the prawns and squid, mixing them well.

4 Toss in the noodles and mix thoroughly. Add the soy sauce and kecap manis, then the mustard leaves and beansprouts.

5 Pour in the beaten eggs and stir them rapidly into the noodles until set, which will take only a few seconds.

6 Season with black pepper, garnish with coriander and serve immediately.

Per Portion Energy 618Kcal/2582kJ; Protein 24.8g; Carbohydrate 100g, of which sugars 1.1g; Fat 12.9g, of which saturates 2.1g; Cholesterol 217mg; Calcium 96mg; Fibre 0.5g; Sodium 717mg.

AROMATIC INDIAN PILAFF WITH PEAS

THIS FRAGRANT, VERSATILE RICE DISH IS OFTEN SERVED AS PART OF AN ELABORATE MEAL AT INDIAN FESTIVALS AND CELEBRATORY FEASTS, WHICH INCLUDE SEVERAL MEAT AND VEGETABLE CURRIES, A YOGURT DISH, AND CHUTNEYS. ON OCCASION, GROUND TURMERIC OR GRATED CARROT IS ADDED FOR AN EXTRA SPLASH OF COLOUR. SPRINKLE THE PILAFF WITH CHOPPED FRESH MINT AND CORIANDER, IF YOU LIKE, OR WITH ROASTED CHILLI AND COCONUT.

SERVES FOUR

INGREDIENTS
 350g/12oz/1¾ cups basmati rice
 45ml/3 tbsp ghee or 30ml/2 tbsp
  vegetable oil and a little butter
 1 cinnamon stick
 6–8 cardamom pods, crushed
 4 cloves
 1 onion, halved lengthways and
  sliced
 25g/1oz fresh root ginger, peeled
  and grated
 5ml/1 tsp sugar
 130g/4½oz fresh peas, shelled
 5ml/1 tsp salt

1 Rinse the rice in several changes of water, until the water runs clear. Put the rice in a bowl, cover with plenty of water and leave to soak for about 30 minutes. Drain thoroughly.

2 Heat the ghee, or oil and butter, in a heavy pan. Stir in the cinnamon stick, cardamom and cloves. Add the onion, ginger and sugar, and fry until golden.

3 Add the peas, followed by the rice, and stir for 1 minute to coat the grains in ghee.

4 Pour in 600ml/1 pint/2½ cups water with the salt, stir once and bring the liquid to the boil.

5 Reduce the heat and allow to simmer gently for 15–20 minutes, until all the liquid has been absorbed. Stir the rice occasionally just to check that it is not sticking to the bottom of the pan.

6 Turn off the heat. Remove the lid and cover the pan with a clean dish towel, then replace the lid to keep the towel in place. Leave to steam for a further 10 minutes. Spoon the rice on to a serving dish.

VARIATION
This Indian pilaff can be made using diced carrot or beetroot (beet), or chickpeas instead of peas. Instead of turmeric, you can add a little tomato paste to give the rice a red tinge.

Per Portion Energy 451Kcal/1880kJ; Protein 8.9g; Carbohydrate 75.7g, of which sugars 2.6g; Fat 12.2g, of which saturates 5.4g; Cholesterol 0mg; Calcium 28mg; Fibre 1.8g; Sodium 328mg.

FISH AND SHELLFISH

Seafood is one of the greatest glories of the cuisines of Singapore, as a huge variety of tropical fish and shellfish are daily hauled from the seas and rivers and sold in the wet markets set up in every town and village. The dishes range from elegantly steamed whole fish, scented with ginger and other aromatics in the Chinese style, to Singapore's famous specialities, fish head curry and chilli crab.

BRAISED GROUPER <u>IN</u> BLACK BEAN SAUCE

GROUPER IS ONE OF THE MOST DESIRABLE FISH ON ACCOUNT OF ITS RICH FLAVOUR AND MEATY TEXTURE. TRADITIONALLY, BRAISED FISH IS COOKED WHOLE, HEAD AND ALL, AND ONLY THE MOST INEDIBLE FINS ARE REMOVED. SOME RESTAURANT CHEFS DEEP-FRY THE FISH BEFORE BRAISING IT AS IT LOOKS MORE IMPRESSIVE AND, WHEN COOKED, STAYS IN SHAPE BETTER.

SERVES FOUR

INGREDIENTS

   1 grouper, about 450g/1lb
   oil for deep-frying (optional)
   30ml/2 tbsp chopped spring onions
    (scallions)
   fresh coriander (cilantro) sprigs,
    to garnish
For the sauce
   30ml/2 tbsp black bean sauce
   15ml/1 tbsp oyster sauce
   10ml/2 tsp garlic purée
   10g/2 tsp ginger purée
   5ml/1 tsp sugar
   2.5ml/½ tsp ground black pepper
   30ml/2 tbsp sesame oil
   60ml/4 tbsp Chinese wine
   15ml/1 tbsp cornflour (cornstarch),
    to thicken (optional)

1 Gut and clean the fish but leave the head on. Trim off the fins with scissors and cut off half the tail if it protrudes too much from the pan you are going to cook it in.

2 Heat enough oil for deep-frying in a wok or large pan and fry the grouper until golden brown if you wish.

VARIATION
For a spicy version, season the sauce with a little chilli powder.

3 Blend all the sauce ingredients with 400ml/14fl oz/1²/₃ cups water and mix well. Bring to the boil in a wok or deep pan and cook for 2 minutes. Add the whole fish and simmer, uncovered, for 10 minutes.

4 Spoon the sauce over the fish from time to time as it cooks, but do not turn the fish over as it might break.

5 Serve the fish hot, garnished with fresh coriander. If you wish to thicken the sauce a little, mix 15ml/1 tbsp cornflour with a little water and stir it into the sauce for the last 2 minutes of cooking.

COOK'S TIP
Don't worry if you don't like the thought of gutting the fish – just ask your fishmonger to do it for you. You could also use fillets rather than a whole fish if you prefer it without the head and tail.

Per portion Energy 173Kcal/727kJ; Protein 14.5g; Carbohydrate 8.8g, of which sugars 5.2g; Fat 7.4g, of which saturates 1.2g; Cholesterol 26mg; Calcium 38mg; Fibre 0.2g; Sodium 274mg.

STINGRAY WINGS WITH CHILLI SAMBAL

CHARGRILLED STINGRAY IS A VERY POPULAR STREET SNACK IN SINGAPORE. THE STALLS SELLING GRILLED CHICKEN WINGS AND SATAY OFTEN SERVE STINGRAY WINGS ON A BANANA LEAF WITH A GENEROUS SPOONFUL OF CHILLI SAMBAL. THE COOKED FISH IS EATEN WITH FINGERS, OR CHOPSTICKS, BY TEARING OFF PIECES AND DIPPING THEM IN THE SAMBAL.

SERVES FOUR

INGREDIENTS
    4 medium-sized stingray wings, about
        200g/7oz, rinsed and patted dry
    salt
    4 banana leaves, about 30cm/
        12in square
    2 fresh limes, halved
For the chilli sambal
    6–8 red chillies, seeded and chopped
    4 garlic cloves, chopped
    5ml/1 tsp shrimp paste
    15ml/1 tbsp tomato purée (paste)
    15ml/1 tbsp palm sugar (jaggery)
    juice of 2 limes
    30ml/2 tbsp vegetable or groundnut
        (peanut) oil

1 First make the chilli sambal. Using a mortar and pestle or food processor, grind the chillies with the garlic to form a paste. Beat in the shrimp paste, tomato purée and sugar. Add the lime juice and bind with the oil.

2 Prepare a charcoal grill. Rub each stingray wing with a little chilli sambal and place them on the rack. Cook for 3–4 minutes on each side, until tender. Sprinkle with salt and serve on banana leaves with the remaining chilli sambal and the limes.

Per Portion Energy 195Kcal/823kJ; Protein 30.4g; Carbohydrate 4.5g, of which sugars 4.5g; Fat 6.3g, of which saturates 0.7g; Cholesterol 0mg; Calcium 83mg; Fibre 0.1g; Sodium 249mg.

FISH HEAD CURRY

THE ORIGINS OF THIS SINGAPORE STREET DISH HAVE BECOME BLURRED WITH TIME. SOME SAY IT CAME WITH IMMIGRANTS FROM KERALA IN SOUTH INDIA; OTHERS CLAIM AN INDIAN CHEF CREATED IT IN SINGAPORE IN THE 1950S OR '60S. IT IS SAID THAT THE BEST FISH HEAD CURRY, PRIZED FOR THE SUCCULENT CHEEKS, IS STILL FOUND AT COFFEE SHOPS IN SINGAPORE.

SERVES TWO

INGREDIENTS
    30ml/2 tbsp ghee or vegetable oil
    10ml/2 tsp brown mustard seeds
    5ml/1 tsp fenugreek seeds
    5ml/1 tsp cumin seeds
    a handful of curry leaves
    15ml/1 tbsp palm sugar (jaggery)
    30ml/2 tbsp tamarind pulp, soaked
      in 150ml/½ pint/⅔ cup water and
      strained for juice
    600ml/1 pint/2½ cups coconut milk
    1 large fresh fish head, such as red
      snapper (about 900g/2lb), cleaned
    5 okra, halved diagonally
    2 large tomatoes, skinned, seeded
      and quartered
    salt and ground black pepper
    steamed rice and pickles, to serve
For the spice paste
    8 shallots, chopped
    6 garlic cloves, chopped
    4 red chillies, seeded and chopped
    50g/2oz fresh root ginger, peeled
      and chopped
    25g/1oz fresh turmeric, chopped
    1 lemon grass stalk, trimmed and
      chopped
    30ml/2 tbsp fish curry powder

COOK'S TIP
Any large fish head, such as salmon, grouper or tuna, can be used.

1 To make the spice paste, grind all the ingredients together using a mortar and pestle or food processor.

2 Heat the ghee or oil in a wok or heavy pan. Stir in the mustard seeds, fenugreek and cumin seeds along with the curry leaves. Fry until the mustard seeds begin to pop and then stir in the spice paste.

3 Fry the spice paste until fragrant, then stir in the sugar, followed by the tamarind juice and coconut milk.

4 Bring to the boil, reduce the heat and add the fish head. Simmer gently for 10 minutes, then add the okra and tomatoes. Simmer for another 10 minutes or until the fish head is cooked. Season the sauce to taste and serve the fish head curry with steamed rice and pickles.

Per Portion Energy 417Kcal/1760kJ; Protein 42.2g; Carbohydrate 30.4g, of which sugars 29.1g; Fat 15.2g, of which saturates 2.7g; Cholesterol 74mg; Calcium 231mg; Fibre 2.7g; Sodium 497mg.

SOUR RAY FISH CURRY

RAYS ARE A FAVOURITE FOOD IN SINGAPORE. THIS FISH IS CARTILAGINOUS, SO IT DOESN'T HAVE THE FINE BONES THAT CHARACTERIZE OTHER FISH, AND LENDS ITSELF TO SOUR CURRIES VERY WELL. THE RAYS BROUGHT TO MARKET TEND TO BE FAIRLY SMALL. SKATE COMES FROM THE SAME FAMILY, AND SKATE WINGS COULD ALSO BE USED IN THIS DISH VERY SUCCESSFULLY.

SERVES FOUR

INGREDIENTS
  500g/1¼lb ray steaks
  6 sour star fruit
  30ml/2 tbsp tamarind
    concentrate
  350ml/12floz/1½ cups water
  juice of 1 lime
  5ml/1 tsp sugar
  salt
  sweet basil leaves, to garnish
For the spice paste
  2 red chillies, seeded and
    chopped
  8 shallots, chopped
  15g/½oz fresh turmeric
  15g/½oz galangal
  15g/½oz shrimp paste

1 Cut the fish into large pieces and rub them with about 5ml/1 tsp salt. Slice the sour star fruit in half lengthways and discard the pith.

2 Grind the ingredients for the spice paste together with a mortar and pestle, until fine and well blended.

3 In a pan, blend the tamarind with water and lime juice, add the paste and bring to the boil. Simmer for 3 minutes then add the fish and the star fruit and cook for a further 10 minutes.

4 Add salt and sugar to taste and garnish with basil leaves before serving.

Per portion Energy 168Kcal/710kJ; Protein 31.6g; Carbohydrate 6.4g, of which sugars 4.8g; Fat 2g, of which saturates 0.3g; Cholesterol 74mg; Calcium 80mg; Fibre 0.2g; Sodium 339mg.

SOUR FISH CURRY

ALTHOUGH THIS DISH IS SIMILAR IN ESSENCE TO SOUR RAY FISH CURRY, THE SPICE PASTE IS QUITE DIFFERENT, AND IS FRIED FIRST BEFORE IT IS ADDED TO THE SAUCE. A LITTLE COCONUT MILK IS ALSO ADDED TO TEMPER THE TARTNESS OF THE TAMARIND, GIVING THE DISH A MUCH RICHER FLAVOUR. CHOOSE A FISH WITH FIRM, MEATY FLESH, SUCH AS POMFRET OR EVEN SALMON.

SERVES FOUR

INGREDIENTS
  500g/1¼lb thick fish cutlets
  1 aubergine (eggplant)
  2 tomatoes
  30ml/2 tbsp tamarind concentrate
  350ml/12 floz/1½ cups water
  45ml/3 tbsp coconut milk
  5ml/1 tsp sugar
  30ml/2 tbsp vegetable oil
  15ml/1 tbsp chilli oil (optional)
  salt
For the spice paste
  2 dried red chillies, softened in
    warm water, seeded and chopped
  ½ large onion, chopped
  15g/½oz fresh turmeric
  15g/½oz shrimp paste
  3 garlic cloves, chopped

1 Cut the fish into large pieces and rub with about 5ml/1 tsp salt. Slice the aubergine lengthways and cut into half moon shapes. Quarter the tomatoes.

2 To make the spice paste, grind all the ingredients together using a mortar and pestle or a food processor. Heat the oil and fry the paste until it is fragrant.

3 Blend the tamarind concentrate with the water and stir it into the fried spice paste. Add the coconut milk, fish, aubergine and tomato.

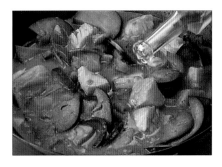

4 Simmer for 8 minutes until the fish is done. Season to taste with salt and sugar. If you wish, add a swirl of chilli oil to give the dish a rich colour.

Per portion Energy 205Kcal/860kJ; Protein 26.5g; Carbohydrate 9.4g, of which sugars 8.9g; Fat 7.1g, of which saturates 1g; Cholesterol 76mg; Calcium 79mg; Fibre 2.7g; Sodium 257mg.

SWEET AND SOUR SNAPPER

THERE MUST BE MORE SWEET AND SOUR RECIPES THAN ANYONE COULD COUNT; VARIATIONS OF THIS IDEA HAVE SPREAD ALL OVER THE WORLD. ESSENTIALLY, THE SWEET AND SOUR TAG REFERS TO THE YIN-YANG BALANCE OF CONTRASTING AND BALANCING FLAVOURS THAT UNDERSCORES MUCH OF CHINESE CUISINE. THIS IS A TROPICAL VERSION, WHICH IS FLAVOURED WITH LIBERAL DASHES OF GARLIC, CHILLIES AND GINGER — BEAUTIFUL, CLEAN FLAVOURS THAT COMPLEMENT THE SNAPPER.

SERVES FOUR

INGREDIENTS
 1 snapper, about 500g/1¼lb
 50g/2oz/¼ cup cornflour
   (cornstarch)
 oil for deep-frying
 2 spring onions (scallions)
For the sauce
 2 garlic cloves
 50g/2oz fresh root ginger,
   peeled
 45ml/3 tbsp plum sauce
 15ml/1 tbsp tomato sauce
 15ml/1 tbsp hoisin sauce
 100ml/3½fl oz/scant ½ cup water
 15ml/1 tbsp vegetable oil
 2 red chillies, seeded

1 Clean and gut the snapper and trim off the fins, but leave the head on. Spread the cornflour on a plate and dip the fish in it to coat. Heat the oil in a wok or large pan and deep-fry the fish for 7–8 minutes, until it is golden brown and crisp and the flesh is cooked.

2 Slice the garlic and ginger into fine strips. Trim the chillies and spring onions and cut into 5cm/2in lengths.

3 For the sauce, mix the plum, tomato and hoi sin sauces with the water.

4 Heat the oil and fry the garlic and ginger until golden. Add the sauce mixture and bring to the boil. Add the sliced chillies and simmer for 1 minute.

5 Arrange the fried fish on a serving plate and pour over the sweet and sour sauce. Garnish with the spring onions and serve immediately.

Per portion Energy 121Kcal/508kJ; Protein 16g; Carbohydrate 3.9g, of which sugars 3.7g; Fat 4.8g, of which saturates 0.7g; Cholesterol 29mg; Calcium 36mg; Fibre 0.1g; Sodium 545mg.

CRAB CURRY

SINGAPORE HAS BEEN THE HOME OF MANY MIGRANT SRI LANKANS FOR OVER A CENTURY, AND THEY ARE THE SOURCE OF ONE OF THE ISLAND'S MOST CAPTIVATING DISHES, SRI LANKAN CRAB CURRY, WHICH IS MADE WITH MOTTLED BLUE CRABS. IN SINGAPORE THERE IS ANOTHER VARIETY OF CRAB CALLED THE THUNDER CRAB. LEGEND HAS IT THAT WHEN ONE NIPS YOU WITH ITS CLAWS, ONLY A THUNDERCLAP WILL MAKE IT RELEASE ITS HOLD.

SERVES FOUR

INGREDIENTS
   8 mottled blue crabs
   60ml/4 tbsp oil
   500m/16 fl oz/2 cups
      coconut milk
   30ml/2 tbsp lime juice
   5ml/1 tsp salt
   30ml/2 tbsp seafood curry powder,
      blended with a little water to
      make a paste
For the spice paste
   ½ large onion, chopped
   5 garlic cloves, chopped
   15ml/1 tbsp grated fresh
      root ginger

1 Remove the shells of the crabs and discard the spongy fibrous tissues.

2 Separate the claws from the bodies if they are large. The smaller legs have very little meat in them, but leave them attached to the bodies as they make good handles for eating with the fingers.

3 Grind the ingredients for the spice paste together using a mortar and pestle or a food processor. Mix the curry powder, blended with water, into the paste.

COOK'S TIP
Blue crabs are available frozen from some Indian stores. If you cannot find them, use any other large, meaty variety that is available from your fishmonger.

4 Heat the oil in a wok or large pan and fry the spice paste for about 3 minutes. Add the coconut milk, lime juice and salt and simmer for 2 minutes.

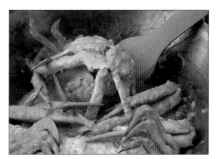

5 Add the crabs to the sauce and cook for about 8 minutes, turning constantly, until the shells have turned completely pink. Serve with rice or bread.

Per portion Energy 288Kcal/1205kJ; Protein 22.5g; Carbohydrate 11.6g, of which sugars 7.1g; Fat 17.4g, of which saturates 2.2g; Cholesterol 55mg; Calcium 86mg; Fibre 0.6g; Sodium 506mg.

PRAWNS IN LIME JUICE

THIS DISH HAS ECHOES OF A DELICIOUS TRADITIONAL BURMESE SALAD IN WHICH THE PRAWNS ARE NOT COOKED BUT ARE STEEPED IN LIME JUICE UNTIL THEY ARE PRACTICALLY PICKLED, IN A TECHNIQUE REMINISCENT OF THE SOUTH AMERICAN CEVICHE. IF YOUR TASTE DOES NOT RUN TO RAW SHELLFISH, BLANCH THE PRAWNS BRIEFLY IN BOILING WATER UNTIL JUST COOKED.

SERVES FOUR

INGREDIENTS

    16 raw tiger prawns (jumbo shrimp)
    4 limes
    3 fresh red chillies, seeded and
      chopped
    3 cloves garlic
    15ml/1 tbsp ginger purée
    15ml/1 tbsp caster (superfine) sugar
    5ml/1 tsp salt
    3 lime leaves, finely shredded

COOK'S TIP
If you can only find ready prepared and cooked tiger prawns in your local supermarket or fishmonger, simply miss out step 1.

1 Shell and devein the prawns. Bring a pan of water to the boil.

2 Drop in the prawns and cook briefly, until they turn pink. Lift them out quickly with a slotted spoon or drain them thoroughly. Be careful that you do not overcook, otherwise they will become tough.

3 Squeeze the limes and grind the chillies until fine. Blend with the lime juice, ginger purée, sugar, salt and shredded lime leaves.

4 Toss the prawns in the sauce and steep for 10 minutes. Chill for an hour and serve on a bed of crisp, shredded lettuce with wedges of lime.

Per portion Energy 55Kcal/234kJ; Protein 9.2g; Carbohydrate 4g, of which sugars 4g; Fat 0.4g, of which saturates 0.1g; Cholesterol 98mg; Calcium 45mg; Fibre 0g; Sodium 587mg.

INDIAN DRY PRAWN AND POTATO CURRY

THIS IS ONE OF THE MOST POPULAR CURRIES AT THE INDIAN STALLS IN SINGAPORE. IN AN INDIAN HOME IT WOULD PROBABLY BE SERVED WITH FLATBREAD, A YOGURT DISH AND CHUTNEY, BUT AT THE NASI KANDAR STALLS IT IS OFTEN ONE OF SEVERAL CURRIED DISHES SERVED WITH RICE. IT'S EQUALLY DELICIOUS MADE WITH PRE-COOKED SWEET POTATOES INSTEAD OF ORDINARY ONES.

SERVES FOUR

INGREDIENTS
    30ml/2 tbsp ghee, or 15ml/1 tbsp
      vegetable oil and 15g/½oz/
      1 tbsp butter
    1 onion, halved lengthways and
      sliced along the grain
    a handful of fresh or dried
      curry leaves
    1 cinnamon stick
    2–3 medium-size waxy potatoes,
      lightly steamed, peeled and diced
    500g/1¼ lb large raw prawns
      (shrimp), peeled and deveined
    200ml/7fl oz/scant 1 cup
      coconut milk
    10ml/2 tsp fennel seeds
    10ml/2 tsp brown mustard seeds
    salt and ground black pepper
    fresh coriander (cilantro) leaves,
      roughly chopped, to garnish
For the spice paste
    4 garlic cloves, chopped
    25g/1oz fresh root ginger, peeled
      and chopped
    2 red chillies, seeded and chopped
    5ml/1 tsp ground turmeric
    15ml/1 tbsp fish curry powder

1 Grind the garlic, ginger and chillies to a coarse paste with a mortar and pestle. Stir in the turmeric and curry powder.

2 Heat the ghee in a heavy pan or earthenware pot. Stir in the onion and fry until golden. Stir in the curry leaves, then the cinnamon stick and the spice paste. Fry until fragrant, then add the potatoes, coating them in the spices. Toss in the prawns and cook for 12 minutes. Stir in the coconut milk and bubble it up to thicken and reduce it. Season with salt and pepper to taste.

3 Roast the fennel and mustard seeds in a small heavy pan until they begin to pop and give off a nutty aroma. Stir them into the curry and serve immediately, sprinkled with coriander.

Per Portion Energy 204Kcal/857kJ; Protein 23.5g; Carbohydrate 13.5g, of which sugars 5.2g; Fat 6.6g, of which saturates 0.9g; Cholesterol 244mg; Calcium 126mg; Fibre 1g; Sodium 299mg.

TOMATO AND CHILLI PRAWNS

IN SINGAPORE THIS IS A SUPREME RESTAURANT DISH CALLED HAR LOKE, WHICH USES PRAWNS IN THEIR SHELLS, COOKED IN A STICKY, SPICY SAUCE. IT IS NEVER MADE WITH SHELLED PRAWNS AS THE SHELLS ACTUALLY SEAL IN THE FULL FLAVOURS OF THE SEAFOOD. IT MAY BE FIDDLY TO PEEL THE PRAWNS WHEN EATING THEM BUT IT IS WELL WORTH THE EFFORT.

SERVES FOUR

INGREDIENTS
    16 raw tiger prawns (jumbo shrimp)
    45ml/3 tbsp vegetable or groundnut
        (peanut) oil
    1 large onion, finely sliced
    2 tomatoes, quartered
For the sauce
    30ml/2 tbsp tomato sauce
    15ml/1 tbsp oyster sauce
    15ml/1 tbsp plum sauce
    15ml/1 tbsp chilli sauce
    90ml/6 tbsp water

1 Snip off about 1cm/½in from the head of each prawn, removing the feelers. Wash and pat dry.

2 In a dry wok, fry the prawns over a high heat for 3 minutes, until they are nearly cooked. Remove and set aside.

3 Add the oil to the wok and fry the onions until soft but not brown. Add the tomatoes and stir-fry for 2 minutes.

4 Mix all the ingredients for the sauce until well blended. Stir the mixture into the vegetables. Return the prawns to the wok and stir constantly until well incorporated and bubbling. The prawns should be completely cooked after about 2 minutes. Serve immediately.

Per portion Energy 166Kcal/693kJ; Protein 10.2g; Carbohydrate 12.2g, of which sugars 10.4g; Fat 8.9g, of which saturates 1.1g; Cholesterol 98mg; Calcium 63mg; Fibre 1.6g; Sodium 225mg.

SINGAPORE CHILLI CRAB

THIS COULD PERHAPS BE DESCRIBED AS SINGAPORE'S SIGNATURE DISH. IT IS AN ALL-TIME FAVOURITE AT HAWKER STALLS AND COFFEE SHOPS, WHERE STEAMING WOKS OF CRAB DEEP-FRYING ARE A COMMON SIGHT. THE CRABS ARE PLACED IN THE MIDDLE OF THE TABLE WITH A BOWL FOR THE DISCARDED PIECES OF SHELL, AND SMALL BOWLS OF WATER FOR CLEANING YOUR FINGERS.

SERVES FOUR

INGREDIENTS
 vegetable oil, for deep-frying
 4 fresh crabs, about 250g/9oz each,
  halved and cleaned
 30ml/2 tbsp sesame oil
 30–45ml/2–3 tbsp chilli sauce
 45ml/3 tbsp tomato ketchup
 15ml/1 tbsp soy sauce
 15ml/1 tbsp sugar
 250ml/8fl oz/1 cup chicken stock
  or water
 2 eggs, beaten
 salt and ground black pepper
 2 spring onions (scallions), finely
  sliced, and fresh coriander
  (cilantro) leaves, finely chopped,
  to garnish
For the spice paste
 4 garlic cloves, chopped
 25g/1oz fresh root ginger, chopped
 4 red chillies, seeded and chopped

COOK'S TIP
To chop a crab in half, killing it instantly, lay it on its back and position a cleaver down the centre line, then strike the back of the cleaver with a mallet.

1 Using a mortar and pestle or food processor, grind the ingredients for the spice paste and set aside.

2 Heat enough oil for deep-frying in a wok or heavy pan. Drop in the crabs and fry until the shells turn bright red. Remove from the oil and drain.

3 Heat the sesame oil in a wok and stir in the spice paste. Fry the paste until fragrant then stir in the chilli sauce, ketchup, soy sauce and sugar.

4 Toss in the fried crab and coat well in the sauce. Pour in the chicken stock or water and bring to the boil.

5 Reduce the heat and simmer for 5 minutes. Season the sauce to taste.

6 Pour in the beaten eggs, stirring the mixture very gently, so the eggs can set in the sauce.

7 Serve immediately, garnished with spring onions and coriander.

Per Portion Energy 276Kcal/1144kJ; Protein 12.1g; Carbohydrate 8.6g, of which sugars 8.1g; Fat 21.7g, of which saturates 3.1g; Cholesterol 126mg; Calcium 23mg; Fibre 0.3g; Sodium 674mg.

POULTRY

Chicken is a staple part of the Singaporean diet. Cooks tend to buy whole birds. The breast portions are sliced for a stir-fry, the rest of the meat used in a curry, and the bones simmered to make a stock. Chicken and duck are the most commonly eaten birds, but goose is also growing in popularity. Free-range chickens are thought to be especially nutritious.

LEMON CHICKEN

A STAR DISH OF CHINESE RESTAURANTS IN SINGAPORE, THIS IS A PERFECT BALANCE OF FLAVOURS BETWEEN THE RICHNESS OF THE BATTERED FRIED CHICKEN AND THE SWEET-SOUR LEMON SAUCE. THERE ARE MANY BRANDS OF LEMON SAUCE IN THE MARKET BUT NOTHING BEATS MAKING YOUR OWN. THE TRICK IN GIVING THE SAUCE A YELLOW COLOUR IS SIMPLY TO USE A LITTLE GROUND TURMERIC.

SERVES FOUR

INGREDIENTS
   2 chicken breasts, skinned
   1 egg, lightly beaten
   30ml/2 tbsp cornflour (cornstarch)
   vegetable or groundnut (peanut) oil
    for deep-frying
   salt
For the sauce
   45ml/3 tbsp lemon juice
   5ml/1 tsp ground turmeric
   15ml/1 tbsp sugar or to taste
   15ml/1 tbsp plum sauce
   175ml/6fl oz water
   5ml/1 tbsp cornflour (cornstarch)

1 Slice each chicken breast across the thickest part to give two thin escalopes (US scallops). Then dip lightly in the beaten egg and coat with cornflour.

2 Heat the oil in a wok or large pan and deep-fry the chicken until golden brown. Keep warm.

3 Mix together all the sauce ingredients, stirring well to avoid lumps. Bring the sauce to a slow simmer in a small pan and cook for 2 minutes. Blend the cornflour with a little water and add, a little at a time, until the sauce is the consistency of pouring (half-and-half) cream. Season to taste with salt.

4 Slice the chicken into 2.5cm/1in strips and place on a serving plate. Pour the sauce over and serve garnished with lemon wedges.

Per portion Energy 231kcal/975kJ; Protein 30.1g; Carbohydrate 13.1g, of which sugars 13.1g; Fat 6.9g, of which saturates 1.2g; Cholesterol 88mg; Calcium 13mg; Fibre 0g; Sodium 76mg.

FUCHOW CHICKEN RICE

*THIS IS A REGIONAL VERSION OF HAINANESE CHICKEN RICE, SOUSED WITH PLENTY OF CHINESE
WINE. IT IS TRADITIONALLY SERVED COLD WITH FRESHLY COOKED JASMINE RICE BUT IT IS JUST
AS GOOD WARM. IN SINGAPORE YOU WILL FIND A FEW RESTAURANTS THAT FEATURE A VARIETY
OF DISHES FROM THIS SUB-PROVINCE OF SOUTH CHINA.*

SERVES FOUR TO SIX

INGREDIENTS
  1 whole chicken (about 1.3kg/3lb)
  60ml/4 tbsp Fuchow rice wine lees or
    Chinese Shao Hsing wine
  30ml/2 tbsp sesame oil
  30ml/2 tbsp ginger purée
  15ml/1 tbsp garlic purée
  5ml/1 tsp salt
  2 spring onions (scallions), trimmed
    and finely sliced

COOK'S TIP
Chinese rice wine is sold in Asian
markets, and is similar to Japanese sake.
Dry sherry or dry vermouth can be
substituted if it is not available.

1 Remove any excess fat from the
chicken and place in a deep dish.
Blend the wine, sesame oil, ginger,
garlic and salt and rub the mixture all
over the chicken, including inside the
body cavity. Leave to stand for at least
30 minutes to absorb the flavours.

2 Steam for 40–50 minutes until the
chicken is tender. Add the spring
onions for the last 5 minutes.

3 Allow the chicken to cool. Chop into
serving pieces and serve cold or warm
with normal jasmine rice.

Per portion Energy 355Kcal/1470kJ; Protein 26.8g; Carbohydrate 0.3g, of which sugars 0.3g; Fat 26g, of which saturates 7g; Cholesterol 139mg; Calcium 16mg; Fibre 0.1g; Sodium 438mg.

Nonya Chicken Curry

The inclusion of potatoes in Nonya chicken curry probably goes back to colonial times, when British plantation owners insisted that their cooks served potatoes with every meal. Not understanding the concept, the Chinese or Nonya cooks they employed would simply add the potatoes directly into the curry.

SERVES FOUR TO SIX

INGREDIENTS
    1 whole chicken (about 1.3kg/3lb)
    2 large potatoes
    30ml/2 tbsp curry powder
    475ml/16fl oz/2 cups
       coconut milk
    30ml/2 tbsp vegetable oil
    25g/1oz ginger purée
    25g/1oz garlic purée
    4 lime leaves
    5ml/1 tsp salt
    5ml/1 tsp sugar
    15ml/1 tbsp lime juice
    30ml/2 tbsp chilli oil
    plain rice, noodles or bread,
       to serve

1 Cut the chicken into serving pieces, removing any excess fat. Wash and pat dry. Peel the potatoes and cut them into chunks.

2 Blend the curry powder with a little of the coconut milk to make a thick paste. Heat the oil in a wok or large pan and fry the potatoes until browned. Lift out and set aside.

COOK'S TIPS
• You could use left-over boiled or roast potatoes in this recipe.
• If you cannot buy ginger and garlic purées, simply pound the root or cloves to a pulp with a mortar and pestle, or process in a blender with a little water.

3 In the oil remaining in the wok, fry the ginger and garlic purée for 2 minutes, until fragrant.

4 Add the curry paste and cook gently until the sauce splits. Add the chicken pieces and sauté until browned. Add the potatoes, coconut milk, lime leaves, salt and sugar. Simmer for 30 minutes.

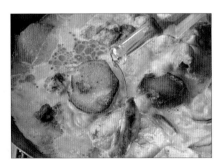

5 Add the lime juice and chilli oil and simmer for another 10–15 minutes until the chicken is tender. Serve with plain rice, noodles or bread.

Per portion Energy 455kcal/1896kJ; Protein 28.6g; Carbohydrate 17.2g, of which sugars 5.6g; Fat 30.7g, of which saturates 7.7g; Cholesterol 139mg; Calcium 47mg; Fibre 0.7g; Sodium 205mg.

CHICKEN OPOR

OPOR IS OF INDONESIAN ORIGIN AND IS A MILDER KIND OF CURRY. TRADITIONALLY, THE SPICE BLEND IS BOILED RATHER THAN BEING PRE-FRIED IN OIL. IT HAS A SUBTLE TASTE OF COCONUT MILK WITH HINTS OF TARTNESS FROM THE SOUR STAR FRUIT AND TAMARIND. AN INTERESTING TOUCH COMES FROM THE FINAL ADDITION OF FRIED GRATED OR DESICCATED COCONUT.

SERVES FOUR

INGREDIENTS
    4 chicken legs
    500ml/16fl oz/2 cups coconut milk
    2 lime leaves
    2 stalks lemon grass
    5ml/1 tsp salt
    30ml/2 tbsp tamarind concentrate
    5ml/1 tsp sugar
    4 sour star fruit (carambola)
    30ml/2 tbsp desiccated (dry
      unsweetened shredded) coconut
For the spice paste
    2 red chillies, seeded and chopped
    5 candlenuts
    ½ large onion, chopped
    3 garlic cloves, chopped
    30ml/2 tbsp ground coriander
    5ml/1 tsp ground fennel
    2 thin slices galangal
    25g/1oz shrimp paste

1 Separate each chicken leg into a thigh and a drumstick, and remove the skin if desired. Put the coconut milk in a large pan, add the pieces of chicken and bring to the boil.

2 Grind the spice paste ingredients until fine and add to the pan with the lime leaves, bruised 5cm/2.5in root ends of the lemon grass, salt, tamarind and sugar. Simmer for 20 minutes.

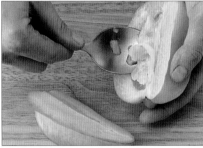

3 Slice each sour star fruit into two lengthways, remove the pith and add to the pan. Simmer for a further 10 minutes.

4 While the chicken is cooking, dry fry the desiccated coconut in another pan until it is light brown. When the chicken is cooked, sprinkle the coconut over the dish and serve immediately.

Per portion Energy 292Kcal/1225kJ; Protein 30.6g; Carbohydrate 13.9g, of which sugars 11.4g; Fat 13.2g, of which saturates 6.4g; Cholesterol 118mg; Calcium 136mg; Fibre 1.3g; Sodium 479mg.

EURASIAN CHICKEN STEW WITH POTATOES

THIS RECIPE IS BELIEVED TO HAVE COME TO THE MALAY PENINSULA WITH THE PORTUGUESE WHO SETTLED IN MELAKA IN THE 16TH CENTURY. IT BECAME A SIGNATURE DISH AMONG THE EURASIAN COMMUNITY IN SINGAPORE, WHO ARE OF MIXED PORTUGUESE, ENGLISH, INDIAN AND CHINESE DESCENT. IT IS NOT FOUND ON RESTAURANT MENUS, ONLY AS A HOME-COOKED DISH.

SERVES FOUR TO SIX

INGREDIENTS
    4 chicken legs
    2 large potatoes
    45ml/3 tbsp vegetable oil
    5 cloves
    7.5cm/3in cinnamon stick
    30ml/2 tbsp Worcestershire sauce
    30ml/2 tbsp dark soy sauce
    475ml/16 fl oz/2 cups water
    15ml/1 tbsp cornflour (cornstarch)
    salt
    crusty bread, to serve

COOK'S TIP
Worcestershire sauce is obviously a British contribution to the dish, added during the 19th century, but the Lea & Perrins recipe was itself derived from flavourings used in Asian cooking.

1 Cut the chicken into serving pieces, removing any excess fat. Peel and quarter the potatoes.

2 Heat the oil in a wok or large pan and sauté the potatoes briefly until browned on all sides. Remove from the pan using a slotted spoon and set aside. Sauté the chicken in the remaining oil until the skin is well browned.

3 Return the potatoes to the pan and stir in the spices, Worcestershire and soy sauces and the water. Season with salt and simmer, covered, for about 35 minutes, until tender.

4 Mix the cornflour with a little water and stir it into the gravy to thicken it. Cook briefly until glossy. Remove the whole spices and serve with bread.

Per portion Energy 238Kcal/1000kJ; Protein 22.2g; Carbohydrate 14.2g, of which sugars 2g; Fat 10.7g, of which saturates 2.1g; Cholesterol 70mg; Calcium 20mg; Fibre 0.7g; Sodium 479mg.

CHICKEN IN RED SAMBAL

THIS IS A POPULAR DISH AMONG SINGAPORE MALAYS, WHO CALL IT AYAM MASAK MERAH. THE METHOD IS IN FACT GENERIC, AND MANY MEAT AND SEAFOOD DISHES ARE COOKED THIS WAY. IT IS AN EVOCATIVE DISH, ALL RED AND VERY FIERY IF YOU USE AS MANY CHILLIES AS MALAY COOKS LIKE TO. HOWEVER, IT CAN BE TEMPERED TO YOUR OWN TASTE, AS MORE OR LESS HEAT DOES NOT ALTER THE INTRINSIC TASTE. IT'S DELICIOUS SERVED WITH BREAD OR RICE.

SERVES FOUR

INGREDIENTS
    4 chicken legs
    150ml/¼ pint/⅔ cup vegetable or
      groundnut (peanut) oil
    15ml/1 tbsp chilli oil
    5ml/1 tsp salt
    10ml/2 tsp sugar
    4 lime leaves, finely shredded
    15ml/1 tbsp tamarind concentrate
    200ml/7fl oz/scant 1 cup water
For the spice paste
    4–6 dried red chillies, soaked in
      warm water until soft, squeezed dry
      and seeded
    ½ large onion, chopped
    4 garlic cloves, chopped
    15ml/1 tbsp shrimp paste
    4 candlenuts

1 Cut each chicken leg into thigh and drumstick joints and trim off any excess fat. Wash and pat dry.

2 Heat the oil in a wok or large pan and fry the chicken pieces, turning several times, until the skin is well browned. Lift out with a slotted spoon and set aside. Remove all but 45ml/3 tbsp of the fat.

3 Grind the ingredients for the spice paste until fine. Fry until fragrant. Add the chilli oil, salt, sugar, lime leaves and tamarind concentrate. Continue to fry for 3 minutes.

4 Add the chicken and water and simmer for 25–30 minutes, until the chicken is done and the sauce is thick.

Per portion Energy 290Kcal/1214kJ; Protein 33.5g; Carbohydrate 3.8g, of which sugars 3.5g; Fat 15.8g, of which saturates 3.1g; Cholesterol 123mg; Calcium 58mg; Fibre 0.2g; Sodium 736mg.

PANDAN-WRAPPED CHICKEN

UNIQUE TO SOUTH-EAST ASIA, THIS DISH HAS MANY REGIONAL VARIATIONS, PRIMARILY IN THAILAND WHERE IT IS OFTEN FEATURED AS AN APPETIZER ON RESTAURANT MENUS. TRY TO FIND PANDAN LEAVES THAT ARE AS WIDE AS POSSIBLE SO THAT YOU CAN MAKE DECENT WRAPS. THE LEAVES PROTECT AND PERFUME THE DELICATE CHICKEN, AS WELL AS KEEPING IN ALL THE FLAVOUR. THERE IS LITTLE NEED TO SERVE A DIPPING SAUCE WITH THIS, AS THE CHICKEN IS STEEPED IN SPICES.

SERVES FOUR TO SIX

INGREDIENTS
   500g/1¼lb skinless, boneless
      chicken breast
   6–8 pandan (screwpine) leaves
   vegetable or groundnut (peanut) oil
      for deep-frying
For the marinade
   15ml/1 tbsp ground coriander
   10ml/2 tsp chilli powder
   5ml/1 tsp ground turmeric
   30ml/2 tbsp lime juice
   5ml/1 tsp sugar

1 Cut the chicken into 3cm/1¹/₂in cubes, wash and dry thoroughly. Mix together the ingredients for the marinade. While the chicken is still damp, blend it with the marinade and set aside for 20 minutes.

2 Cut the pandan leaves into 15cm/6in lengths. Put them into a bowl and pour over boiling water. Leave them for about a minute so that they blanch and soften, and release their perfume.

3 Wrap each piece of chicken in a pandan leaf and secure with cocktail sticks (toothpicks), snipping off any protruding ends.

4 Heat the oil in a wok or large pan, deep-fry the parcels until they are golden brown, and serve for diners to unwrap each piece at the table.

Per portion Energy 199Kcal/832kJ; Protein 21.3g; Carbohydrate 4.4g, of which sugars 2.3g; Fat 10.9g, of which saturates 1.4g; Cholesterol 58mg; Calcium 31mg; Fibre 0.7g; Sodium 54mg.

SOY BRAISED CHICKEN

THIS WAS ORIGINALLY A CLASSIC CANTONESE RESTAURANT DISH, FLAVOURED WITH FIVE-SPICE POWDER, BUT THE NONYA TAKE ON IT, AS IS TYPICAL, INCLUDES A LARGE, BRUISED KNOB OF GALANGAL INSTEAD. IT IS A VERY GOOD DISH TO SERVE WHEN ENTERTAINING, AS IT CAN BE COOKED UP TO A DAY IN ADVANCE AND SIMPLY REHEATED. ALWAYS SERVE IT WITH A SHARP CHILLI, GARLIC AND VINEGAR DIP AND PLENTY OF SLICED CUCUMBER AND RICE.

SERVES SIX TO EIGHT

INGREDIENTS
   1 whole chicken (about 1.3kg/3lb)
   25g/1oz sugar
   90ml/6 tbsp dark soy sauce
   25g/1oz galangal, bruised
   1.5 litres/2½ pints/6¼ cups water
   10ml/2 tsp salt
   15ml/1 tbsp cornflour (cornstarch)
   steamed rice and sliced cucumber,
     to serve

1 Remove any excess fat from the chicken, wash it and pat dry. In a dry, heavy pan, heat the sugar until frothy and caramelized to a rich, dark brown colour. Add the chicken and turn it several times in the pan until well sealed.

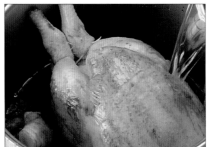

2 Add the soy sauce, galangal and water. Bring to the boil and simmer, covered, for 30 minutes, turning several times so the chicken is evenly cooked.

3 Add salt and continue to cook for another 15–20 minutes until tender. Remove and set aside.

4 Increase the heat and boil until the sauce is well reduced and glossy. Blend the cornflour with a little water and add to the sauce to thicken it.

5 Chop the chicken into bitesize pieces and serve with rice and sliced cucumber, with the sauce on the side.

Per portion Energy 255Kcal/1058kJ; Protein 20.2g; Carbohydrate 5.9g, of which sugars 4.1g; Fat 16.8g, of which saturates 4.9g; Cholesterol 104mg; Calcium 12mg; Fibre 0g; Sodium 883mg.

CORIANDER BRAISED DUCK

THIS GLORIOUS DISH HAS BEEN A NONYA MAINSTAY FOR GENERATIONS. A PRESSURE COOKER IS USEFUL FOR THIS, BUT IF YOU USE ONE YOU SHOULD COOK THE DISH WITHOUT USING PRESSURE FOR THE LAST HALF HOUR TO REDUCE AND CONCENTRATE THE SPICY JUICES THAT CHARACTERIZE THE DISH. IF YOU CAN FIND LENGTHS OF SUGAR CANE, THEY CAN TAKE THE PLACE OF ORDINARY SUGAR FOR A REALLY AUTHENTIC TASTING RESULT.

SERVES SIX TO EIGHT

INGREDIENTS
   1 prepared duck (about 1.5kg/3½lb),
     trimmed of excess fat
   45ml/3 tbsp vegetable oil
   45g/3 tbsp minced (ground) onions
   30g/2 tbsp garlic purée
   30g/2 tbsp ground coriander
   5ml/1 tsp black pepper
   30ml/2 tbsp dark soy sauce
   20cm/8in sugar cane, cut into 6
     pieces or 30ml/2 tbsp sugar
   60ml/4 tbsp finely chopped fresh
     coriander (cilantro)
   2 cinnamon sticks, 10cm/4in long
   6 cloves
   1.5 litres/2½ pints/6 cups water,
     or more

1 Wash the duck and dry it well. Heat the oil in a deep wok or pan and add the onions, garlic purée and coriander. Fry gently for 5 minutes.

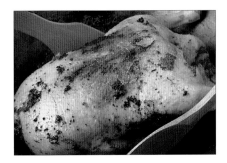

2 Put the duck into the wok or pan and fry for about 10 minutes, turning several times, to brown the skin all over.

3 Stir in all the other ingredients, cover the pan and gently simmer over a very low heat for about 2 hours, until the meat is tender. Alternatively, transfer the duck and other ingredients to a pressure cooker and cook under high pressure for 30 minutes, then de-pressurize and braise for a further 30 minutes.

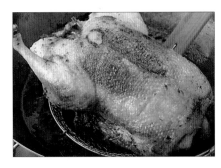

4 Remove the duck from the pan and keep it warm. Raise the heat and bring the sauce to a furious boil to reduce it to a syrupy consistency.

5 Cut the duck into large serving pieces, removing any large bones. Arrange on a serving dish and pour the sauce over it. Serve with plain rice.

Per portion Energy 510Kcal/2120kJ; Protein 17.8g; Carbohydrate 26.9g, of which sugars 26.8g; Fat 47.5g, of which saturates 10.5g; Cholesterol 87mg; Calcium 35mg; Fibre 0.1g; Sodium 380mg.

MEAT

The meat dishes of Singapore divide along religious lines, as the types of meat eaten are subject to the dietary codes of Islam, Hinduism and Buddhism. Pork is a staple of Chinese cooking and appears in many Singapore specialities. Prime cuts are used for speedy stir-fries, for which the meat is usually sliced thinly for quick cooking, while rich, tasty curries call for long, gentle cooking.

STIR-FRIED BEEF IN OYSTER SAUCE

THIS SIMPLE BUT DELICIOUS RECIPE IS OFTEN MADE WITH JUST STRAW MUSHROOMS, WHICH ARE READILY AVAILABLE FRESH IN SOUTH-EAST ASIA, BUT OYSTER MUSHROOMS MAKE A GOOD SUBSTITUTE AND USING A MIXTURE MAKES THE DISH EXTRA INTERESTING.

SERVES FOUR TO SIX

INGREDIENTS
    450g/1lb rump (round) steak
    30ml/2 tbsp soy sauce
    15ml/1 tbsp cornflour (cornstarch)
    45ml/3 tbsp vegetable oil
    15ml/1 tbsp chopped garlic
    15ml/1 tbsp chopped fresh
      root ginger
    225g/8oz/3¼ cups mixed
      mushrooms such as shiitake,
      oyster and straw
    30ml/2 tbsp oyster sauce
    5ml/1 tsp granulated (white) sugar
    4 spring onions (scallions),
      cut into short lengths
    ground black pepper
    2 fresh red chillies, seeded
      and cut into strips,
      to garnish

1 Place the steak in the freezer for 30–40 minutes, until firm, then, using a sharp knife, slice it on the diagonal into long thin strips.

2 Mix together the soy sauce and cornflour in a large bowl. Add the steak, turning to coat well, cover with clear film (plastic wrap) and leave to marinate at room temperature for 1–2 hours.

3 Heat half the oil in a wok or large, heavy frying pan. Add the garlic and ginger and cook for 1–2 minutes, until fragrant. Drain the steak, add it to the wok or pan and stir well to separate the strips. Cook, stirring frequently, for a further 1–2 minutes, until the steak is browned all over and tender. Remove from the wok or pan and set aside.

4 Heat the remaining oil in the wok or pan. Add the shiitake, oyster and straw mushrooms. Stir-fry over a medium heat until golden brown.

5 Return the steak to the wok and mix it with the mushrooms. Spoon in the oyster sauce and sugar, mix well, then add ground black pepper to taste. Toss over the heat until all the ingredients are thoroughly combined.

6 Stir in the spring onions. Tip the mixture on to a serving platter, garnish with the strips of red chilli and serve.

Per portion Energy 171Kcal/717kJ; Protein20g; Carbohydrate 8.3g, of which sugars 5.6g; Fat 6.6g, of which saturates 1.9g; Cholesterol 52mg; Calcium 28mg; Fibre 1.1g; Sodium 343mg.

NONYA SAMBAL PORK

THIS TRADITIONAL DISH IS COOKED MOSTLY WITHOUT WATER, WITH THE RESULT THAT THE PORK IS ALMOST PICKLED. THE ONLY CUT OF PORK TO USE FOR THIS IS BELLY, AS IT HAS THE CORRECT PROPORTION OF LEAN MEAT AND FAT. IT IS WORTH COOKING A LARGE BATCH AS IT KEEPS SO WELL.

SERVES FOUR

INGREDIENTS
  1kg/2¼lb belly pork
  500ml/17fl oz/generous
    2 cups water
  45ml/3 tbsp vegetable oil
  2.5ml/1 tsp salt
  10ml/2 tsp sugar
  6 kaffir lime leaves
  30ml/2 tbsp dark soy sauce
For the spice paste
  1 large onion or 20 shallots,
    roughly chopped
  3 stalks lemon grass, trimmed
    to leave 7.5cm/3in of the
    root end
  10g/¼oz galangal, chopped
  10 dried chillies, soaked until
    soft and seeds removed (optional
    for milder flavour)
  4 garlic cloves, chopped
  40g/1½oz shrimp paste
  8 candlenuts

1 First make the spice blend. Grind all the paste ingredients in a mortar and pestle or food processor until fine.

2 Put the pork in a pan and add the water. Bring to the boil and cook for 15 minutes. Remove the pork and drain well.

COOK'S TIP
When making the spice paste, it will reduce splattering if you process the onions separately first, then add the other spices, as the onion purée will facilitate the grinding process.

3 Holding the meat firmly, insert a sharp knife between the skin and the meat, and remove the skin in one piece.

4 Cut the pork into 3cm/1in wide strips trimming off any excess fat.

5 Heat the oil in a wok or heavy pan and fry the spice paste over low heat for 10 minutes. Do not rush this step.

6 Add the pork and fry over low heat for 10 minutes until evenly browned. Add salt, sugar and soy sauce and continue to fry for 5 minutes, making sure every piece is well coated. The pork will take on a mahogany hue.

7 Remove the central spine of each lime leaf and shred very finely with a sharp knife or scissors. Add the shredded leaves to the pork in the last minutes of frying. Leave to cool before storing in an airtight container, if not serving immediately. It goes very well with sliced cucumber.

Per portion Energy 703Kcal/2917kJ; Protein 49.2g; Carbohydrate 13.3g, of which sugars 8.8g; Fat 50.8g, of which saturates 16.6g; Cholesterol 183mg; Calcium 172mg; Fibre 1.4g; Sodium 5314mg.

PORK RIBS IN BLACK BEAN SAUCE

BLACK BEANS AND BLACK BEAN SAUCE ARE ALMOST EXCLUSIVE TO MALAYSIAN AND SINGAPORE CHINESE COOKING, AND GO PARTICULARLY WELL WITH PORK. BOILING THE RIBS FIRST ENSURES A MORE SUCCULENT TEXTURE AND THE MEAT ABSORBS THE SEASONINGS BETTER.

SERVES FOUR

INGREDIENTS
8 large meaty pork spare ribs
500ml/17 fl oz/generous 2 cups water
30ml/2 tbsp light soy sauce
15g/½oz fresh root ginger
3 garlic cloves
2 red chillies
45ml/3 tbsp sesame oil
30ml/2 tbsp black bean sauce

1 Cut each rib into 6cm/2½in pieces. Bring the water to the boil in a wok or heavy pan and add the soy sauce. Add the ribs and cook for 20 minutes. Drain, reserving the stock for another dish.

2 Finely chop the ginger, garlic and chillies. Blend the sesame oil with the black bean sauce and add the ginger, garlic and chillies. Pour the mixture over the cooked ribs in a shallow dish and leave to marinate for several hours.

3 When ready to cook, lift the ribs out of the marinade and arrange them in a shallow dish. Put the dish in a bamboo steamer, cover and steam the ribs for about 15 minutes until they are heated through and tender.

Per portion Energy 722Kcal/3012kJ; Protein 61.8g; Carbohydrate 2.6g, of which sugars 1g; Fat 51.9g, of which saturates 18.1g; Cholesterol 215mg; Calcium 59mg; Fibre 0.7g; Sodium 897mg.

FENG

PORTUGUESE EURASIANS EAT FENG AT CHRISTMAS. TRADITIONALLY MADE WITH OFFAL, THIS CURRY REPRESENTS A MIX OF MALAY AND PORTUGUESE CULINARY TRADITIONS. IF YOU ARE NOT A FAN OF OFFAL, USE LEAN PORK FROM THE HIND LEG — THIS VERSION OF THE CURRY IS POPULAR IN SINGAPORE.

SERVES FOUR

INGREDIENTS

  1kg/2¼lb mixed pork offal
    (such as liver, lungs, intestines
    and heart), thoroughly washed and
    cleaned and trimmed
  30ml/2 tbsp vegetable oil
  50g/2oz fresh root ginger, peeled
    and shredded
  15–30ml/1–2 tbsp white wine
    vinegar or rice vinegar
  salt
  bread or steamed rice, to serve
For the spice paste
  8 shallots, chopped
  4 garlic cloves, chopped
  25g/1oz fresh root ginger, peeled
    and chopped
  30ml/2 tbsp coriander seeds
  10ml/2 tsp cumin seeds
  10ml/2 tsp fennel seeds
  10ml/2 tsp black peppercorns
  5ml/1 tsp ground turmeric

1 First make the spice paste. Using a mortar and pestle or food processor, grind the shallots, garlic and ginger to a paste.

2 In a heavy pan, dry-roast the coriander, cumin and fennel seeds with the peppercorns until they emit a nutty aroma. Grind the roasted spices to a powder and stir them into the spice paste with the ground turmeric.

3 Put the offal, except the liver, in a pan with water to cover. Bring to the boil, lower the heat and cook for 40 minutes.

4 Add the liver and cook for a further 5 minutes, until all the offal is tender. Drain the offal but reserve the cooking broth. Cut the offal into bitesize pieces.

5 Heat the oil in a wok or earthenware pot. Stir in the ginger and fry until crisp. Lift the ginger out and set aside.

6 Stir the spice paste into the oil and fry until fragrant. Add the offal and toss it to brown lightly. Stir in the vinegar over a high heat and season. Stir in half the crispy fried ginger and scatter the rest over the top.

7 Serve the dish hot with fresh, crusty bread or steamed rice and some simple steamed green vegetables.

Per Portion Energy 444Kcal/1858kJ; Protein 53.6g; Carbohydrate 7.2g, of which sugars 1.4g; Fat 13.3g, of which saturates 5.9g; Cholesterol 650mg; Calcium 21mg; Fibre 0.4g; Sodium 218mg.

PORK RIBS IN PANDAN LEAVES

THE SINGAPOREANS HAVE A PENCHANT FOR SWEET TASTES AND PORK IS OFTEN MARRIED WITH SWEET FLAVOURINGS. THEY LOVE PORK COATED IN HONEY AND GRILLED, STIR-FRIED OR ROASTED. IN THIS CHINESE-STYLE SINGAPORE DISH, THE PORK IS MARINATED IN HONEY AND WESTERN FLAVOURINGS, BEFORE BEING WRAPPED IN LONG, THIN PANDAN LEAVES AND DEEP-FRIED. SERVE THESE PORK RIBS AS AN APPETIZER OR AS A MAIN COURSE WITH STIR-FRIED RICE OR NOODLES.

SERVES FOUR TO FIVE

INGREDIENTS
   675g/1½lb meaty pork ribs, cut into
     bitesize pieces
   25 pandan (screwpine) leaves
   vegetable oil, for deep-frying
   2 limes, cut into wedges, to serve
For the marinade
   6 shallots, chopped
   4 garlic cloves, chopped
   25g/1oz fresh root ginger, peeled
     and chopped
   30ml/2 tbsp clear honey
   45ml/3 tbsp Worcestershire sauce
   30ml/2 tbsp tomato ketchup
   30ml/2 tbsp sour plum sauce
   15ml/1 tbsp sesame oil

1 First make the marinade. Using a mortar and pestle or food processor, grind the shallots, garlic and ginger to a smooth paste. Beat in the honey, Worcestershire sauce, tomato ketchup, sour plum sauce and sesame oil, mixing thoroughly until fully blended.

2 Put the pork ribs in a shallow dish and smear the marinade all over them. Set aside for 2–3 hours.

3 Lay the pandan leaves on a flat surface and place a marinated pork rib in the centre of each one. Tie a tight knot over each rib so that the ends poke out.

4 Heat the vegetable oil in a large wok or heavy pan for deep-frying and fry the wrapped ribs in batches for about 4–5 minutes until cooked.

5 Serve immediately, still wrapped in the leaves, with lime wedges for squeezing, so that each diner can open their own parcels.

COOK'S TIP
Pandan leaves lend a unique fragrance to this dish, but if they are not available you can substitute banana or bamboo leaves cut into strips. Pandan leaves are always used when slightly withered, as the fresh leaves have very little scent.

Per Portion Energy 299Kcal/1250kJ; Protein 25.5g; Carbohydrate 4.1g, of which sugars 3.8g; Fat 20.3g, of which saturates 7.3g; Cholesterol 89mg; Calcium 24mg; Fibre 0.2g; Sodium 182mg.

TIFFIN PORK CHOPS

THIS DISH IS STEEPED IN SINGAPORE'S COLONIAL HISTORY. TIFFIN IS BELIEVED TO DERIVE FROM MEALS ORDERED FROM INDIAN COOKS BY BRITISH ARMY OFFICERS, WHICH WERE DELIVERED IN METAL TIFFIN CARRIERS. WHEN THESE MEN MARRIED AND SET UP HOME, THEY WOULD HIRE HAINANESE COOKS AND PROBABLY INSTRUCTED THEM TO COOK SIMILAR ALL-IN-ONE DISHES, WITH PORK AND POTATOES IN GRAVY MADE WITH TOMATO KETCHUP AND THE VERY BRITISH WORCESTERSHIRE SAUCE.

SERVES FOUR

INGREDIENTS

    4 thick boneless pork chops
    10ml/2 tsp cornflour (cornstarch)
    60ml/4 tbsp vegetable or groundnut
      (peanut) oil
    2 large potatoes, peeled and cut into
      5mm/¼in slices
    1 large onion, sliced
    30ml/2 tbsp Worcestershire
      sauce
    30ml/2 tbsp tomato ketchup
    200ml/7fl oz/scant 1 cup water
    2.5ml/½ tsp ground black pepper
    mushy peas and extra Worcestershire
      sauce, to serve (optional)

1 Slice the pork chops horizontally to make thin escalopes, to facilitate cooking. Beat them with a meat mallet to tenderize them and dust them lightly with cornflour.

2 Heat 15ml/1 tbsp of the oil in a wok or heavy pan and fry the pieces of pork quickly on both sides until they are lightly browned. Remove to a plate and set aside.

3 Heat the remaining oil in the pan and fry the sliced onion until soft and golden but not brown. Remove and set aside.

4 Meanwhile, blend the Worcestershire sauce with the tomato ketchup, water and pepper and stir until smooth.

5 Fry the sliced potatoes in the onion cooking oil in a single layer, cooking them in batches if necessary, until they are browned on both sides and partially cooked. Remove them with a slotted spoon and drain on kitchen paper.

6 Return the pork, onion and potatoes to the pan and add the sauce. Bring to a quick boil and cook, stirring, until the sauce is rich and glossy. If you want to serve the dish in British colonial style, serve with mushy peas and more Worcestershire sauce on the side.

Per portion Energy 517Kcal/2164kJ; Protein 51.6g; Carbohydrate 29.6g, of which sugars 10.1g; Fat 22.1g, of which saturates 6.5g; Cholesterol 165mg; Calcium 60mg; Fibre 2.5g; Sodium 354mg.

PORK CURRY

ALTHOUGH MOST CURRIES ORIGINATE FROM THE INDIAN OR INDONESIAN KITCHEN, CHINESE COOKS HAVE CREATED THEIR OWN VERSION, WHICH SITS SOMEWHERE BETWEEN THE TWO. GENERALLY MILD, THIS CURRY RESEMBLES JAPANESE-STYLE CURRY IN THAT IT IS SWEET RATHER THAN HOT. COCONUT MILK IS RARELY PRESENT IN CHINESE COOKING – UNLESS IT IS USED BY NONYAS WHO ARE OF CHINESE STOCK – AND THIS IS ONE OF THE FEW RECIPES THAT INCLUDES IT.

SERVES FOUR

INGREDIENTS

    500g/1¼lb boneless pork chops
    4 tomatoes
    2 large potatoes
    45ml/3 tbsp vegetable oil
    30ml/2 tbsp mild curry powder
    15g/½oz ground ginger
    400ml/14 fl oz/1⅔ cups
      coconut milk
    10ml/2 tsp sugar
    15ml/1 tbsp light soy sauce
    15ml/1 tbsp lime juice
    steamed rice, to serve

1 Slice the pork horizontally into thin escalopes, then cut into 5cm/2in squares. Tenderize with a meat mallet. Skin, quarter and deseed the tomatoes.

2 Peel the potatoes and cut them into chunks. Heat the oil in a wok or heavy pan and fry the potatoes over high heat, turning them constantly so that they brown lightly on all sides. This will help to prevent them breaking up while being simmered with the pork. Remove them with a slotted spoon and drain on kitchen paper.

3 Blend the curry powder to a paste with a little water. Stir the ginger into the remaining oil and add the curry paste. Fry for 4 minutes until fragrant.

4 Add the coconut milk, sugar and soy sauce. Bring to the boil, add the pork and potatoes and simmer for 15 minutes. Add the lime juice and serve.

Per portion Energy 373Kcal/1569kJ; Protein 30.9g; Carbohydrate 30.4g, of which sugars 13g; Fat 15.2g, of which saturates 3.3g; Cholesterol 79mg; Calcium 68mg; Fibre 2.3g; Sodium 490mg.

INDIAN DRY MUTTON CURRY

IN SINGAPORE, A REFERENCE TO MUTTON USUALLY MEANS GOAT MEAT, AND NOT SHEEP MEAT AS IN THE WEST. SHEEP ARE NOT REARED IN ASIA, SO WHEN LAMB IS REQUIRED IT IS USUALLY IMPORTED FROZEN. MOST INDIANS IN THE REGION ARE EITHER HINDUS WHO ESCHEW BEEF OR MUSLIMS WHO DO NOT EAT PORK. GOAT MEAT CAN BE TOUGH AND NEEDS LONG SIMMERING, BUT HAS A MUCH STRONGER FLAVOUR THAN LAMB. THE BEST CUTS ARE BONELESS CHOPS. THIS DISH CAN BE SERVED WITH RICE.

SERVES FOUR

INGREDIENTS
    500g/1¼lb mutton chops
    5ml/1 tsp cumin seeds
    15ml/1 tbsp chilli powder
    15ml/1 tbsp ground coriander
    5ml/1 tsp ground turmeric
    75ml/5 tbsp water
    45ml/3 tbsp oil
    250ml/8fl oz/1 cup thin
      coconut milk
    salt and ground black pepper
    small bunch of fresh coriander
      (cilantro), to garnish

1 Cut the mutton into 3cm/1¼in cubes. Soak the cumin seeds in water, then drain them and crush coarsely using a mortar and pestle or in a blender or food processor.

2 Blend the cumin with the chilli powder, ground coriander, turmeric and a generous grinding of pepper, and add a little water to make a paste.

3 Stir the paste into the mutton and leave to marinate for 30 minutes.

COOK'S TIP
Thin coconut milk is recommended for this slow-cooked dish, as thick coconut milk can render down to oil over long cooking. Canned coconut milk is quite thick, so thin down the contents of the can with ½ can water.

4 Heat the oil and fry the mutton for about 4 minutes, until fragrant. Add the coconut milk and salt and simmer over low heat, covered, for about 1 hour.

5 The curry should be almost dry when cooked. You may have to top up with coconut milk if the evaporation rate is high, so have extra standing by.

Per portion Energy 581Kcal/2403kJ; Protein 19.6g; Carbohydrate 5.7g, of which sugars 3.1g; Fat 53.7g, of which saturates 23.2g; Cholesterol 96mg; Calcium 41mg; Fibre 0g; Sodium 148mg.

SINGAPORE FIVE-SPICE MEAT ROLLS

A GREAT FAVOURITE AT THE CZE CHA HAWKER STALLS IN SINGAPORE, THESE DEEP-FRIED STEAMED ROLLS ARE DELICIOUS WITH A DIPPING SAUCE. WRAPPED IN TRADITIONAL TOFU SHEETS, THEY CAN BE SERVED AS A SNACK, OR EATEN AS PART OF A LIGHT MEAL WITH RICE, PIQUANT SAUCE AND A SALAD.

SERVES FOUR

INGREDIENTS
  225g/8oz minced (ground) pork
  150g/5oz fresh prawns (shrimp),
    peeled and finely chopped
  115g/4oz water chestnuts,
    finely chopped
  15ml/1 tbsp light soy sauce
  15ml/1 tbsp dark soy sauce
  15ml/1 tbsp sour plum sauce
  7.5ml/1½ tsp sesame oil
  10ml/2 tsp five-spice powder
  5ml/1 tsp glutinous rice flour
    or cornflour (cornstarch)
  1 egg, lightly beaten
  4 fresh tofu sheets, 18–20cm/
    7–8in square, soaked in
    warm water
  vegetable oil, for deep-frying
  chilli oil, for drizzling
  soy sauce mixed with chopped
    chillies, to serve

1 Put the minced pork, chopped prawns and water chestnuts in a bowl. Add the soy sauces, sour plum sauce and sesame oil and mix well.

2 Stir in the five-spice powder, glutinous rice flour or cornflour, and egg. Mix well to blend thoroughly.

3 Lay the tofu sheets on a flat surface and divide the pork mixture between them, placing spoonfuls towards the edge nearest you.

COOK'S TIP
Tofu sheets are available in Chinese and Asian markets and large supermarkets, but if you cannot find them, try making these rolls with Asian rice sheets or even with filo pastry.

4 Pull the nearest edge up over the filling, tuck in the sides and roll into a log, just like a spring roll. Moisten the last edge with a little water to seal the roll. Repeat to make four rolls.

5 Fill a wok one-third of the way up with water and place a bamboo steamer in it. Bring the water to the boil and place the tofu rolls in the steamer. Cover and steam for 15 minutes.

6 Remove the steamed rolls with tongs and place them on a clean dish towel.

7 Heat enough oil for deep-frying in a wok. Fry the steamed rolls in batches until crisp and golden. Drain them on kitchen paper.

8 Serve the rolls hot, whole or sliced. Drizzle them with chilli oil and serve with a little dipping bowl of soy sauce mixed with finely chopped red chillies or a ready-made chilli dip.

Per Portion Energy 339Kcal/1413kJ; Protein 24.4g; Carbohydrate 12.5g, of which sugars 2.7g; Fat 21.6g, of which saturates 4.2g; Cholesterol 158mg; Calcium 343mg; Fibre 1.2g; Sodium 65mg.

VEGETABLES AND SALADS

The tropical climate of Singapore means that most vegetables are available all year round. Cool, colourful salads act as a foil for spicy snacks and curries, and often incorporate fresh fruits such as pineapple and mango as well as crunchy vegetables. Exotic local vegetables such as water spinach and bamboo shoots are tossed into stir-fries and briefly cooked to retain all their colour and flavour, while Indian influences are revealed in slow-cooked vegetable curries.

KANGKUNG AND SWEET POTATO LEMAK

RARELY FOUND OUTSIDE THE NONYA HOME, THIS IS AN UNUSUAL DISH IN THAT IT IS ONE OF THE VERY FEW SPICY DISHES TO FEATURE SWEET POTATO. A ROOT VEGETABLE ASSOCIATED WITH THE REGION'S HUNGRY POSTWAR YEARS, IT HAS NOW GAINED RESPECT AS A GOOD CARBOHYDRATE THAT ALSO HAS A DISTINCTIVE SWEETNESS WITHOUT BEING CLOYING. WITH THE KANGKUNG AND RICH, COCONUT MILK-BASED SAUCE, IT MAKES A VERY SATISFYING MAIN COURSE.

SERVES FOUR

INGREDIENTS
  225g/8oz kangkung
  150g/5oz sweet potato
  45ml/3 tbsp vegetable or groundnut
    (peanut) oil
  400ml/14fl oz/1⅔ cups coconut milk
  5ml/1 tsp salt
  5ml/1 tsp sugar
For the spice paste
  5 candlenuts
  8 shallots
  15g/½oz shrimp paste
  15ml/1 tbsp dried shrimps,
    soaked until soft
  15g/½oz fresh turmeric, chopped
  3 garlic cloves, chopped
  5 red chillies, chopped
  steamed rice, to serve

1 Wash the kangkung well. Slice the stalks thinly and tear off the leaves in small bunches. Peel the sweet potato and cut into chunks, wash and dry.

2 Grind together all the ingredients for the spice paste. Heat the oil in a wok or heavy pan and fry the ground spices for 3 minutes, until fragrant.

3 Add the coconut milk, kangkung and sweet potatoes. Bring to the boil and add salt and sugar.

4 Cook for 10-15 minutes until the sweet potato is soft. Kangkung cooks very quickly but is unique in that it never becomes mushy with long simmering. Serve with rice.

Per portion Energy 194Kcal/812kJ; Protein 7.7g; Carbohydrate 20.1g, of which sugars 11.7g; Fat 9.9g, of which saturates 1.4g; Cholesterol 38mg; Calcium 244mg; Fibre 2.8g; Sodium 1023mg.

Deep-fried Aubergine with Garlic Sauce

This dish is often served at the rice stalls in Singapore as an accompaniment to coconut rice. Many cooks at the stalls, and in the home, make up batches of different sambals to be stored and used for quickly made dishes like this one. At the hawker stalls the aubergines are generally deep-fried, but they could be baked in the oven instead. Serve as a snack with bread or as a side dish with rice or grilled meats.

SERVES TWO TO FOUR

INGREDIENTS

6 shallots, chopped
4 garlic cloves, chopped
2 red chillies, seeded and chopped
1 lemon grass stalk, trimmed
   and chopped
5ml/1 tsp shrimp paste
15ml/1 tbsp sesame oil
15–30ml/1–2 tbsp soy sauce
7.5ml/1½ tsp sugar
2 slender, purple aubergines
   (eggplants), partially peeled in
   strips and halved lengthways
vegetable oil, for deep-frying
To garnish
1 green chilli, seeded and finely
   chopped
a small bunch each of fresh mint and
   coriander (cilantro), stalks removed,
   finely chopped

1 Using a mortar and pestle or food processor, grind the shallots, garlic, chillies and lemon grass to a paste. Beat in the shrimp paste and mix well.

2 Heat the sesame oil in a small wok or heavy pan. Stir in the spice paste and cook until fragrant and brown. Stir in the soy sauce and sugar and cook until smooth. Remove from the heat.

3 Heat enough oil for deep-frying in a wok or heavy pan. Drop in the aubergine halves and fry until tender. Drain on kitchen paper, then press down the centre of each half to make a dip or shallow pouch. Arrange the aubergine halves on a plate and smear or brush them with the spicy sauce. Garnish with the chopped green chilli, mint and coriander leaves, and serve at room temperature.

Per Portion Energy 158Kcal/654kJ; Protein 1.6g; Carbohydrate 6.5g, of which sugars 5.1g; Fat 14.2g, of which saturates 1.8g; Cholesterol 0mg; Calcium 24mg; Fibre 2.7g; Sodium 271mg.

STIR-FRIED BITTER GOURD WITH SAMBAL

ACCORDING TO THE PRINCIPLES OF TRADITIONAL CHINESE MEDICINE, ANY FOOD THAT HAS A BITTER EDGE IS GOOD FOR CLEANSING THE LIVER AND CAN HELP TO BRING DOWN RAISED BLOOD PRESSURE. BITTER GOURD, ALSO KNOWN AS BITTER MELON, FULFILS THIS ROLE BRILLIANTLY. ITS TANGINESS IS APPETIZING AS WELL AS BENEFICIAL, AND THE PIQUANT SAMBAL ENHANCES THE TASTE GREATLY.

SERVES FOUR

INGREDIENTS
    1 whole bitter gourd
    30ml/2 tbsp oil
    30ml/2 tbsp sambal goreng (fried
        chilli paste)
    100ml/3½fl oz/scant ½ cup water
    5ml/1 tsp sugar
    15ml/1 tbsp lime juice

1 Cut the bitter gourd in half down its length. Use a spoon to scoop out the pith and red seeds. Slice into half moon pieces each 1cm/½in wide.

2 Bring a pan of water to the boil and blanch the bitter gourd for 2 minutes. Drain. This removes some bitterness and shortens the cooking time.

3 Heat the oil and fry the sambal goreng for just 1 minute, as it is already cooked. Add the pieces of gourd and stir-fry rapidly for 3 minutes.

4 Add the water, sugar and lime juice and continue to stir for another 2 minutes until the ingredients are well blended. Serve hot.

Per portion Energy 72Kcal/299kJ; Protein 1.3g; Carbohydrate 3.9g, of which sugars 3.3g; Fat 5.8g, of which saturates 0.8g; Cholesterol 0mg; Calcium 41mg; Fibre 1.3g; Sodium 1mg.

STEAMED WINTER MELON WITH BARLEY

*TO THE CHINESE, ALL PARTS OF THE WINTER MELON, INCLUDING THE SEEDS, RIND, PULP AND JUICE,
ARE REGARDED AS MEDICINAL AND GOOD FOR THE TREATMENT OF URINARY AND KIDNEY DISEASES.
THE SKIN ALSO HAS ANTISEPTIC AND ANALGESIC PROPERTIES. IN THIS RECIPE THE SKIN OF THE MELON
CAN BE USED AS THE CONTAINER FOR A SIMPLE, WARMING SOUP THICKENED WITH BARLEY.*

SERVES FOUR

INGREDIENTS

   1 whole winter melon (about
     1.2kg/2½lb)
   45ml/3 tbsp hulled or pearl barley
   600ml/1 pint/2½ cups very
     hot water
   15ml/1 tbsp preserved winter melon
     (tung chai)
   5ml/1 tsp salt
   15ml/1 tbsp sesame oil
   ground black pepper

1 Soak the barley in enough water to cover for several hours, or boil for 20 minutes, to reconstitute the grain. Drain and discard the water.

2 If using the skin as a bowl, cut a slice about 4cm/1½in from the top of the melon and reserve. Cut around the edge of the melon flesh, about 2.5cm/1in away from the outer skin. Cut out the pith, leaving a deep hollow in the melon (be careful not to puncture the skin).

3 Place the whole melon in a deep dish, or use a deep bowl, and place in a steamer that has a high-domed lid. Pour the hot water into the bowl or shell and stir in the reserved melon flesh, barley, salt and sesame oil. Replace the melon "lid" or cover the bowl, and steam for 30 minutes.

4 At the end of the cooking time the barley grains should be plump and very soft. Season to taste with black pepper.

5 Serve the winter melon while piping hot, straight from the steamer in its steaming dish. Diners can eat the filling, then scoop out flesh from the sides of the melon shell for eating afterwards.

Per portion Energy 125Kcal/529kJ; Protein 2.2g; Carbohydrate 23.4g, of which sugars 14g; Fat 3.2g, of which saturates 0.4g; Cholesterol 0mg; Calcium 35mg; Fibre 1g; Sodium 569mg.

THREE VEGETABLES STIR-FRY

STIR-FRYING HAS CAUGHT ON ALL OVER THE WORLD IN RECENT DECADES, AND MOST CHEFS WILL ACKNOWLEDGE THAT IT IS ARGUABLY THE HEALTHIEST WAY TO COOK VEGETABLES. WHEN STIR-FRIED THEY TASTE CRUNCHY AND RETAIN THEIR NUTRIENTS, WHICH ARE MOSTLY SOLUBLE. THEY ALSO TAKE ONLY MINUTES TO PREPARE, AND YOU CAN USE ANY VEGETABLES THAT YOU LIKE FOR THIS DISH.

SERVES FOUR

INGREDIENTS

- 100g/3¾oz mangetouts (snow peas)
- 100g/3¾oz baby corn cobs
- 100g/3¾oz water chestnuts
- 30ml/2 tbsp vegetable oil
- 15ml/1 tbsp sesame oil
- 2 garlic cloves
- 30ml/2 tbsp yellow bean sauce

1 Top and tail the mangetouts. Cut each corn cob into two and slice the water chestnuts into thin rings.

2 Heat the oils in a wok or large, heavy pan. Crush the garlic and fry in the oil for 1 minute. Add all the prepared vegetables and the yellow bean sauce and stir-fry rapidly over high heat so that all the pieces cook evenly.

3 Sprinkle a scant 30ml/1 tbsp of water over the vegetables, just to moisten them – this dish is not meant to be water-logged – stir for 30 seconds and serve immediately.

Per portion Energy 103Kcal/427kJ; Protein 2.9g; Carbohydrate 3.9g, of which sugars 2g; Fat 8.6g, of which saturates 1.1g; Cholesterol 0mg; Calcium 24mg; Fibre 1.8g; Sodium 316mg.

COCONUT VEGETABLE STEW

THIS DISH IS OF INDONESIAN ORIGIN BUT HAS BEEN ENTRENCHED IN THE CUISINES OF SINGAPORE FOR A LONG TIME. THERE IS A POPULAR COMPRESSED RICE ROLL DISH CALLED LONTONG THAT IS OFTEN CUT INTO BITESIZE PIECES AND SERVED WITH A VEGETABLE STEW OF THIS KIND, SOMETIMES WITH CHICKEN ADDED. THE VEGETABLES YOU USE FOR THE STEW ARE A MATTER OF PERSONAL CHOICE.

SERVES FOUR

INGREDIENTS

   1 large potato
   1 large carrot
   150g/5oz cabbage
   1 green or purple aubergine
     (eggplant)
   45ml/3 tbsp vegetable oil
   500ml/17fl oz/generous 2 cups
     coconut milk
   5ml/1 tsp salt
   5ml/1 tsp sugar
For the spice paste
   4 candlenuts
   8 shallots, chopped
   10ml/2 tsp shrimp paste
   15ml/1 tbsp dried shrimp,
     soaked until soft
   15g/½oz fresh turmeric, chopped
   3 garlic, cloves
   5 dried red chillies, softened in
     warm water

1 Peel the potatoes and cut them into thick slices. Peel the carrot and cut into batons about 1cm/½in thick and 7.5cm/3in long. Cut the cabbage into chunky pieces and slice the aubergine into 1cm/½in thick rounds.

COOK'S TIP
As well as the vegetables listed here, you could use courgettes (zucchini), French (green) or long (snake) beans for this dish.

2 Grind all the ingredients for the spice paste together until smooth. Heat the oil in a pan and fry the spice paste for 2 minutes or until fragrant. Add the coconut milk, salt and sugar.

3 Stir in all the vegetables. Return the liquid to the boil then lower the heat and cover the pan. Simmer the stew for 30 minutes, checking often to see that the vegetables do not get overcooked. Serve the stew hot with rice or bread.

Per portion Energy 120Kcal/502kJ; Protein 1.8g; Carbohydrate 8.3g, of which sugars 8g; Fat 9.2g, of which saturates 1.3g; Cholesterol 0mg; Calcium 44mg; Fibre 3.4g; Sodium 107mg.

POTATO CURRY WITH YOGURT

VARIATIONS OF THIS SIMPLE INDIAN CURRY ARE POPULAR AT THE HAWKER STALLS IN SINGAPORE, WHERE IT IS SERVED WITH FLATBREAD. SOME SINGAPORE COFFEE SHOPS EVEN SERVE IT FOR BREAKFAST. IT IS DELICIOUS ON ITS OWN, SERVED WITH YOGURT AND A SPICY PICKLE OR CHUTNEY.

SERVES FOUR

INGREDIENTS

6 garlic cloves, chopped
25g/1oz fresh root ginger, peeled
  and chopped
30ml/2 tbsp ghee, or 15ml/1 tbsp oil
  and 15g/½oz/1 tbsp butter
6 shallots, halved lengthways and
  sliced along the grain
2 green chillies, seeded and
  finely sliced
10ml/2 tsp sugar
a handful of fresh or dried
  curry leaves
2 cinnamon sticks
5–10ml/1–2 tsp ground turmeric

15ml/1 tbsp garam masala
500g/1¼lb waxy potatoes, cut into
  bitesize pieces
2 tomatoes, peeled, seeded
  and quartered
250ml/8fl oz/1 cup Greek (US
  strained plain) yogurt
salt and ground black pepper
5ml/1 tsp red chilli powder, and fresh
  coriander (cilantro) and mint leaves,
  finely chopped, to garnish
1 lemon, quartered, to serve

COOK'S TIP
This recipe also works well with sweet
potatoes, butternut squash or pumpkin,
all of which absorb the flavours.

1 Using a mortar and pestle or a food processor, grind the garlic and ginger to a coarse paste. Heat the ghee in a heavy pan and stir in the shallots and chillies, until fragrant. Add the garlic and ginger paste with the sugar, and stir until the mixture begins to colour.

2 Stir in the curry leaves, cinnamon sticks, turmeric and garam masala, and toss in the potatoes, turning them over to make sure they are well coated in the spice mixture.

3 Pour in just enough cold water to cover the potatoes. Bring to the boil, then reduce the heat and simmer until the potatoes are just cooked – they should still have a bite to them. Season with salt and pepper to taste.

4 Gently toss in the tomatoes to heat them through. Fold in the yogurt so that it is streaky rather than completely mixed in. Sprinkle with the chilli powder, coriander and mint. Serve immediately from the pan, with lemon to squeeze over it and flatbread for scooping it up.

Per Portion Energy 231Kcal/967kJ; Protein 6.7g; Carbohydrate 26.2g, of which sugars 7.4g; Fat 12.4g, of which saturates 4.1g; Cholesterol 0mg; Calcium 110mg; Fibre 2g; Sodium 63mg.

BRAISED TOFU WITH MIXED MUSHROOMS

FOUR DIFFERENT KINDS OF MUSHROOMS ARE INCLUDED IN THIS RECIPE AND THEY FLAVOUR THE TOFU BEAUTIFULLY TO MAKE A PERFECT VEGETARIAN MAIN COURSE. THE DISH HAS AN UNMISTAKABLY CHINESE TASTE, THANKS TO THE FLAVOURS OF SOY SAUCE, GINGER AND CHINESE RICE WINE.

SERVES FOUR

INGREDIENTS
- 350g/12oz tofu (bean curd)
- 2.5ml/½ tsp sesame oil
- 10ml/2 tsp light soy sauce
- 15ml/1 tbsp vegetable oil
- 2 garlic cloves, finely chopped
- 2.5ml/½ tsp grated fresh root ginger
- 115g/4oz/1 cup fresh shiitake mushrooms, stalks removed
- 175g/6oz/1½ cups fresh oyster mushrooms
- 115g/4oz/1 cup drained, canned straw mushrooms
- 115g/4oz/1 cup button mushrooms, cut in half
- 15ml/1 tbsp Chinese rice wine or dry sherry
- 15ml/1 tbsp dark soy sauce
- 90ml/6 tbsp vegetable stock
- 5ml/1 tsp cornflour (cornstarch), blended to a paste with a little cold water
- salt and ground white pepper
- 2 spring onions (scallions), shredded

1 Put the tofu in a dish and sprinkle with the sesame oil, light soy sauce and a large pinch of pepper. Leave to marinate for 10 minutes, then drain and cut into 2.5 x 1cm/1 x ½in pieces.

2 Heat the vegetable oil in a wok. When it is very hot, fry the chopped garlic and ginger for a few seconds, taking care to stir it and prevent it from burning. Add all the mushrooms and stir-fry for 2 minutes.

3 Stir in the wine or sherry, soy sauce and stock, with salt, if needed, and pepper. Simmer for 4 minutes.

4 Stir in the cornflour paste and cook, stirring, until thickened.

5 Carefully add the pieces of bean curd, toss gently to coat thoroughly and simmer for 2 minutes. Scatter the shredded spring onions over the mixture, transfer to a serving dish and serve immediately.

COOK'S TIP
In Asian dishes, aim to use a good, light vegetable oil for frying rather than a fruity or heavy variety such as extra-virgin olive oil. Corn, soya, peanut or pure olive oil are all good for stir-frying as they can be heated to high temperatures without smoking and tainting the food.

Per portion Energy 116Kcal/483kJ; Protein 9.6g; Carbohydrate 1.7g, of which sugars 1g; Fat 7.5g, of which saturates 1g; Cholesterol 0mg; Calcium 456mg; Fibre 1.4g; Sodium 456mg.

AVIAL <u>WITH</u> ROASTED COCONUT

ORIGINALLY FROM SOUTHERN INDIA, THIS DELICIOUS DISH HAS FOUND ITS WAY INTO MANY MALAY HOMES. IN SINGAPORE, IT IS SERVED IN SOME COFFEE SHOPS AND AT THE INDIAN AND MALAY STALLS, WHERE IT IS OFTEN AMONG A SELECTION OF DISHES OFFERED TO ACCOMPANY RICE. FOR VEGETARIAN HINDUS, IT IS A POPULAR EVERYDAY DISH OR A TASTY SNACK, SERVED WITH INDIAN FLATBREAD. MADE WITH FIRM VEGETABLES, ROOTS AND GOURDS, ALL CUT INTO LONG BITESIZE PIECES, IT IS SUBSTANTIAL AND FLEXIBLE — CHOOSE YOUR OWN ASSORTMENT OF VEGETABLES, SUCH AS PUMPKIN, BUTTERNUT SQUASH, WINTER MELON, YAMS, AUBERGINES OR BEANS.

SERVES FOUR

INGREDIENTS
2–3 green chillies, seeded and
   chopped
25g/1oz fresh root ginger, peeled
   and chopped
5–10ml/1–2 tsp roasted cumin seeds
10ml/2 tsp sugar
5–10ml/1–2 tsp ground turmeric
1 cinnamon stick
5ml/1 tsp salt
2 carrots, cut into bitesize sticks
2 sweet potatoes, cut into
   bitesize sticks
2 courgettes (zucchini), partially
   peeled in strips, seeded and cut
   into bitesize sticks
1 green plantain, peeled and cut into
   bitesize sticks
a small coil of long (snake) beans or
   a handful of French or green
   beans, cut into bitesize
   lengths
a handful fresh curry leaves
1 fresh coconut, grated
250ml/8fl oz/1 cup
   Greek (US strained plain)
   yogurt
salt and ground black pepper

1 Using a mortar and pestle or food processor, grind the chillies, ginger, roasted cumin seeds and sugar to a paste.

2 In a large, heavy pan, bring 450ml/15fl oz/scant 2 cups water to the boil. Stir in the turmeric, whole cinnamon stick and salt.

3 Add the carrots and cook for 1 minute. Add the sweet potatoes and cook for 2 minutes. Add the courgettes, plantain and beans and cook for a further 2 minutes.

4 Reduce the heat and stir in the spice paste and curry leaves.

5 Cook gently for 4–5 minutes, or until the vegetables are tender – but not soft and mushy – and the liquid volume has greatly reduced.

COOK'S TIPS
• Choose live yogurt if you can find it – the beneficial bacteria help to maintain good digestion.
• Plantains may be found in larger supermarkets, but a better selection of fruit and vegetables for cooking non-European cuisine is often available in small Caribbean or Asian stores.

6 Gently stir in half the grated coconut. Take the pan off the heat and fold in the yogurt. Season to taste with salt and pepper.

7 Quickly toast the remaining grated coconut in a heavy pan over a high heat, until nicely browned. Meanwhile, heat serving plates in the oven.

8 Sprinkle a little toasted coconut over the vegetables in the pan, then divide the avial between individual plates.

9 Serve hot, with the rest of the coconut and warmed flatbreads on the side for people to help themselves.

Per Portion Energy 419Kcal/1753kJ; Protein 9.9g; Carbohydrate 47.7g, of which sugars 19.4g; Fat 23g, of which saturates 16.9g; Cholesterol 0mg; Calcium 176mg; Fibre 9g; Sodium 104mg.

ROJAK

ORIGINALLY FROM INDONESIA, ROJAK HAS BEEN SO WELL INTEGRATED INTO THE CUISINE OF SINGAPORE THAT THERE IS EVEN AN INDIAN VERSION. AS THIS RECIPE IS SO FLEXIBLE, YOU CAN USE ANY COMBINATION OR FRUIT AND VEGETABLES AND MAKE THE SAUCE AS FIERY AS YOU LIKE.

SERVES FOUR TO SIX

INGREDIENTS

1 jicama (sweet turnip), peeled and finely sliced
1 small cucumber, partially peeled and finely sliced
1 green mango, peeled and finely sliced
1 star fruit (carambola), finely sliced
4 slices fresh pineapple, cored
half a pomelo, separated into segments, with membrane removed
a handful of beansprouts, washed and drained
fresh mint leaves, to garnish
For the sauce
225g/8oz/2 cups roasted peanuts
4 garlic cloves, chopped
2–4 red chillies, seeded and chopped
10ml/2 tsp shrimp paste, dry-roasted in a pan over a high heat
15ml/1 tbsp tamarind paste
30ml/2 tbsp palm sugar (jaggery)
salt

1 First make the sauce. Using a mortar and pestle or food processor, grind the peanuts with the garlic and chillies to a coarse paste. Beat in the roasted shrimp paste, tamarind paste and sugar. Add enough water to make a thick, pouring sauce, and stir until the sugar has dissolved. Add salt to taste.

2 Arrange all the sliced fruit and vegetables on a plate, with the beansprouts scattered over the top. Drizzle the sauce over the salad and garnish with mint leaves. Serve as an accompaniment to grilled (broiled) meats and spicy dishes, or on its own as a healthy snack.

Per Portion Energy 330Kcal/1381kJ; Protein 12.9g; Carbohydrate 28g, of which sugars 25.1g; Fat 19.3g, of which saturates 3.4g; Cholesterol 13mg; Calcium 114mg; Fibre 6.3g; Sodium 416mg.

CUCUMBER AND SHALLOT SALAD

IN SINGAPORE, THIS LIGHT, REFRESHING SALAD IS SERVED WITH INDIAN FOOD ALMOST AS OFTEN AS COOLING MINT-FLAVOURED CUCUMBER RAITA. IT CAN BE MADE AHEAD OF TIME AND KEPT IN THE REFRIGERATOR. SERVE IT AS A SALAD OR A RELISH.

SERVES FOUR

INGREDIENTS

    1 cucumber, peeled, halved
       lengthways and seeded
    4 shallots, halved lengthways and
       sliced finely along the grain
    1–2 green chillies, seeded and sliced
       finely lengthways
    60ml/4 tbsp coconut milk
    5–10ml/1–2 tsp cumin seeds,
       dry-roasted and ground to
       a powder
    salt
    1 lime, quartered, to serve

1 Slice the cucumber halves finely and sprinkle with salt. Set aside for about 15 minutes. Rinse well and drain off any excess water.

2 Put the cucumber, shallots and chillies in a bowl. Pour in the coconut milk and toss well. Sprinkle most of the roasted cumin over the top. Just before serving, toss the salad again, season with salt, and sprinkle the rest of the roasted cumin over the top. Serve with lime wedges to squeeze over the salad.

Per Portion Energy 17Kcal/68kJ; Protein 0.7g; Carbohydrate 3.3g, of which sugars 2.7g; Fat 0.1g, of which saturates 0g; Cholesterol 0mg; Calcium 19mg; Fibre 0.7g; Sodium 15mg.

BRIDAL SALAD

ACTUALLY MORE A FIERY SAMBAL THAN A SALAD, DESPITE ITS NAME, THIS DISH IS DE RIGUEUR AT TRADITIONAL PERANAKAN AND MALAY WEDDINGS. IT HAS MUCH SYMBOLIC MEANING TO ENSURE THAT THE BRIDE WILL GO ON TO HAVE A GOOD, FERTILE LIFE AND BEAR HER HUSBAND MANY OFFSPRING. IT MAKES VERY GOOD EATING AT ANY TIME, EVEN IF IT IS TONGUE-SEARINGLY HOT.

SERVES FOUR

INGREDIENTS
  10 fresh red chillies
  10 fresh green chillies
  45ml/3 tbsp vegetable oil
  4 kaffir lime leaves
  350ml/12fl oz/1½ cups
    coconut milk
  30ml/2 tbsp lime juice
  5ml/1 tsp salt
  5ml/1 tsp sugar
For the spice paste
  ½ large onion, chopped
  4 garlic cloves, chopped
  15ml/1 tbsp shrimp paste
  6 candlenuts

COOK'S TIP
You can add 200g/7oz of shelled prawns (shrimp) for a richer dish.

1 Remove the stalks from the chillies and slice each into two lengthways. Scoop out the seeds and remove some of the pith, where most of the heat is concentrated.

2 Heat the oil in a wok or heavy pan and fry the chillies for 2 minutes until they are slightly shrivelled. Remove them and set aside to cool.

3 Grind the ingredients for the spice paste until smooth. In the remaining oil, fry the spice paste for 2 minutes. Add the lime leaves, coconut milk, lime juice, salt and sugar and stir over medium heat for 3 minutes.

4 Return the fried chillies to the pan and stir for 1 minute. Serve with plain steamed rice.

Per portion Energy 137Kcal/570kJ; Protein 5.8g; Carbohydrate 8g, of which sugars 7g; Fat 9.3g, of which saturates 1.2g; Cholesterol 19mg; Calcium 106mg; Fibre 0.4g; Sodium 758mg.

WINTER MELON PACHADI

Some varieties of pachadi and raita dishes, originating in Southern India, are designed to cool the palate and aid digestion when eating hot, spicy food. These yogurt-based dishes are made with cooling vegetables and herbs, such as okra, courgette, spinach, pumpkin, cucumber with mint, and this refreshing winter melon.

SERVES FOUR

INGREDIENTS

225g/8oz winter melon, peeled, seeded and diced
5ml/1 tsp ground turmeric
5ml/1 tsp red chilli powder
300ml/½ pint/1¼ cups Greek (US strained plain) yogurt
2.5ml/½ tsp salt
2.5ml/½ tsp sugar
15g/½oz fresh root ginger, peeled and grated
1 green chilli, seeded and finely chopped
15ml/1 tbsp vegetable oil
1.5ml/¼ tsp ground asafoetida
5ml/1 tsp brown mustard seeds
8–10 dried curry leaves
1 dried red chilli, seeded and roughly chopped

COOK'S TIP

In Singapore, cooling Indian dishes like pachadi are often served at the Indian and Malay stalls and coffee shops to balance the hot curries and spicy grilled dishes. In many Indian households, the pachadi is made a day or two in advance, so that the flavours mingle.

1 Put the diced winter melon in a heavy pan with the turmeric and chilli powder and pour in enough water to just cover it. Bring to the boil and cook gently, uncovered, until the winter melon is tender and all the water has been absorbed or evaporated.

2 In a bowl, beat the yogurt with the salt and sugar until smooth and creamy. Add the ginger and green chilli, and fold in the warm winter melon.

3 Heat the oil in small heavy pan. Stir in the asafoetida and the brown mustard seeds.

4 As soon as the mustard seeds begin to pop, stir in the curry leaves and dried chilli. When the chilli darkens, add the spices to the yogurt and mix thoroughly.

5 Allow the pachadi to reach room temperature before serving.

Per Portion Energy 127Kcal/527kJ; Protein 5.1g; Carbohydrate 5.3g, of which sugars 5.3g; Fat 10.5g, of which saturates 4.2g; Cholesterol 0mg; Calcium 120mg; Fibre 0.2g; Sodium 316mg.

SWEET SNACKS

The abundant tropical fruit available throughout the year
is usually eaten at the end of a meal or as a refreshing
snack during the day, either as it is, or turned into cooling
water ices or refreshing fruit juices. The inhabitants of
Singapore also enjoy a variety of very sweet snacks, rich
with coconut cream and eggs, and fragrant with pandan
and spices. Baked, fried or steamed, they are sold at the
hawker stalls and eaten warm.

LYCHEE SORBET

Sorbets are lovely alternatives to ice cream, especially for those who are watching their weight. They are easy to make and you can use any soft fruit. They make delightful taste cleansers between courses but are equally satisfying as a dessert at the end of a meal. Many kinds of tropical fruit make successful sorbets, including limes, mangoes and papayas, but fragrant lychee sorbet remains a favourite.

SERVES FOUR

INGREDIENTS
  500g/1¼lb lychees, peeled and
    stoned (pitted)
  500ml/17fl oz/generous 2 cups
    lychee syrup
  juice of 2 limes
  fresh mint leaves, to decorate

COOK'S TIPS
Lychee syrup is available from supermarkets. If fresh lychees are not available you can make this sorbet using canned lychees and the syrup from the can. You can add 250ml/8fl oz/1 cup of single (light) cream or natural (plain) yogurt when processing the second time for an even smoother sorbet.

1 Process the lychees in a food processor with half the syrup until you get a smooth purée. Mix in the remaining syrup and the lime juice.

2 Pour into a large plastic container or ice cream tub, cover and place in the coldest part of the freezer.

3 Freeze the mixture for several hours until slushy. Return to the processor and blend until light and creamy. Return to the container and re-freeze until firm, preferably overnight.

4 Serve in individual bowls, decorated with a mint leaf or two.

Per portion Energy 249kcal/1064kJ; Protein 1.4g; Carbohydrate 64.7g, of which sugars 64.7g; Fat 0.1g, of which saturates 0g; Cholesterol 0mg; Calcium 31mg; Fibre 0.9g; Sodium 4mg.

JELLIED MANGO PUDDINGS

LIGHT AND SOPHISTICATED, THESE INDIVIDUAL JELLIED MANGO PUDDINGS MAKE DELIGHTFUL AND ATTRACTIVE DESSERTS. SERVED WITH A SELECTION OF TROPICAL FRUITS SUCH AS THOSE SUGGESTED BELOW, THEY ADD A REFRESHING TOUCH TO THE END OF ANY MEAL, ESPECIALLY A SPICY ONE. YOU ARE MORE LIKELY TO FIND ELEGANT LITTLE PUDDINGS OF THIS KIND IN THE DIM SUM RESTAURANTS OF SINGAPORE THAN AS A SWEET SNACK AT A HAWKER STALL.

SERVES FOUR

INGREDIENTS
- 750ml/1¼ pints/3 cups coconut milk
- 150g/5oz/¾ cup sugar
- 15ml/1 tbsp powdered gelatine
- 1 egg yolk
- 1 large, ripe mango, stoned (pitted) and puréed
- 4 slices ripe jackfruit or pineapple, quartered
- 1 banana, cut into diagonal slices
- 1 kiwi fruit, sliced
- 4 lychees, peeled
- 2 passion fruit, split open, to decorate

1 In a heavy pan, heat the coconut milk with the sugar, stirring all the time, until it has dissolved. Add the gelatine and keep stirring until it has dissolved. Remove from the heat. Beat the egg yolk with the mango purée.

2 Add the purée to the coconut milk and stir until smooth. Spoon the mixture into individual, lightly oiled moulds and leave to cool. Place them in the refrigerator and leave for 2–3 hours, until set.

VARIATION
The tangy fruitiness of mango is particularly delicious in these jellied puddings, but you could substitute papaya, banana, durian or avocado.

3 To serve, arrange the fruit on individual plates, leaving enough room for the jellies. Dip the base of each mould briefly into hot water, and then invert the puddings on to the plates. Lift off the moulds and decorate with passion fruit seeds.

Per Portion Energy 305Kcal/1300kJ; Protein 2.9g; Carbohydrate 72.6g, of which sugars 72g; Fat 2.4g, of which saturates 0.8g; Cholesterol 50mg; Calcium 109mg; Fibre 3g; Sodium 216mg.

GINGER AND COCONUT MILK CUSTARDS

DELICATE AND WARMING, GINGER CUSTARD IS A FAVOURITE AMONG THE CHINESE AND PERANAKANS IN SINGAPORE. OFTEN SERVED WARM, STRAIGHT FROM THE STEAMER, THE INDIVIDUAL CUSTARDS ARE ENJOYED AS A SWEET MID-AFTERNOON SNACK OR EVEN LATE AT NIGHT.

SERVES FOUR

INGREDIENTS
  115g/4oz fresh root ginger,
    finely chopped
  400ml/14fl oz/1⅔ cups coconut milk
  60ml/4 tbsp sugar
  2 egg whites

1 Using a mortar and pestle or a blender or food processor, grind or blend the root ginger to a fine paste.

2 Press the ginger paste through a fine sieve (strainer), to extract the juice. Discard the pulp.

3 Fill a wok one-third of the way up with water. Place a bamboo steamer in the wok, bring the water to the boil and reduce the heat to low.

4 In a bowl, whisk the coconut milk, sugar and egg whites with the ginger juice until the mixture is smooth and the sugar has dissolved.

5 Pour the custard into four individual heatproof bowls and place them in the steamer. Cover and steam for about 15–20 minutes, until set.

6 Remove the bowls from the steamer and leave the custards to cool. They can be served while still slightly warm. Alternatively, cover them with clear film (plastic wrap) once they are completely cool and place in the refrigerator overnight to firm up. Serve the custards chilled or at room temperature.

Per Portion Energy 89Kcal/380kJ; Protein 2g; Carbohydrate 20.8g, of which sugars 20.8g; Fat 0.4g, of which saturates 0.2g; Cholesterol 0mg; Calcium 50mg; Fibre 0.3g; Sodium 159mg.

BLACK GLUTINOUS RICE PUDDING

ALSO KNOWN AS BLACK STICKY RICE, BLACK GLUTINOUS RICE HAS LONG DARK GRAINS AND A NUTTY TASTE REMINISCENT OF WILD RICE. THIS BAKED PUDDING HAS A DISTINCT CHARACTER AND FLAVOUR ALL OF ITS OWN, AS WELL AS AN INTRIGUING APPEARANCE.

SERVES FOUR TO SIX

INGREDIENTS
175g/6oz/1 cup black or white
glutinous rice
30ml/2 tbsp soft light brown sugar
475ml/16fl oz/2 cups coconut milk
250ml/8fl oz/1 cup water
3 eggs
30ml/2 tbsp granulated (white) sugar

1 Combine the glutinous rice and brown sugar in a pan. Pour in half the coconut milk and the water.

2 Bring to the boil, reduce the heat to low and simmer, stirring occasionally, for 15–20 minutes, or until the rice has absorbed most of the liquid. Preheat the oven to 150°C/300°F/Gas 2.

3 Spoon the rice into a large ovenproof dish or divide it among individual ramekins.

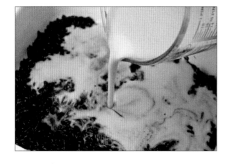

4 Beat the eggs with the remaining coconut milk and sugar. Strain the egg mixture into a jug (pitcher), then pour it evenly over the par-cooked rice.

5 Place the dish or ramekins in a roasting pan. Carefully pour in enough hot water to come halfway up the sides of the dish or ramekins.

6 Cover with foil and bake for about 35–60 minutes, or until the custard has set. Serve warm or cold.

COOK'S TIP
Throughout South-east Asia, black glutinous rice is usually used for sweet dishes, while its white counterpart is more often used in savoury recipes.

Per portion Energy 135Kcal/568kJ; Protein 1.7g; Carbohydrate 31.8g, of which sugars 17.4g; Fat 0.3g, of which saturates 0g; Cholesterol 0mg; Calcium 247mg; Fibre 0g; Sodium 2mg.

STICKY COCONUT RICE IN BANANA LEAVES

SWEET AND SAVOURY STICKY RICE COOKED IN BANANA LEAVES IS COMMON FARE IN THE MARKETS AND AT THE HAWKER STALLS THROUGHOUT SOUTH-EAST ASIA. IN THIS RECIPE, SLICED BANANA IS ADDED TO STEAMED RICE TO MAKE THIS SWEET TREAT PARTICULARLY MOIST AND DELICIOUS.

6 Place the banana leaf squares on a flat surface. Spread 30ml/2 tbsp of rice in the centre of each, in the shape of a rectangle. Place a few overlapping banana slices on top and form a sandwich with another 30ml/2 tbsp rice. Fold in the two short ends, and then fold over the wider flaps to form a bundle. Secure the bundle with string or a cocktail stick (toothpick).

7 Refill the wok one-third of the way up with water. Place the bundles in the bamboo steamer, cover with the lid and steam for 1 hour. Serve the bundles hot, straight from the steamer, with a spoonful of coconut cream and a dusting of icing sugar, or leave them to cool in the banana leaves and serve at room temperature as a sweet snack.

SERVES FOUR

INGREDIENTS

115g/4oz/generous ½ cup white sticky rice, well rinsed in several changes of water, soaked in plenty of water for 6 hours and drained
400ml/14fl oz/1⅔ cups coconut milk
60ml/4 tbsp palm sugar (jaggery)
banana leaves, cut into pieces, roughly 20cm/8in square
2 bananas, cut into diagonal slices
salt
coconut cream and icing (confectioners') sugar, to serve

1 Fill a wok one-third of the way up with water and place a bamboo steamer inside it. Bring the water to the boil. Alternatively use an electric steamer.

2 Place a piece of muslin (cheesecloth), dampened in warm water, over the steamer rack.

3 Spread the sticky rice on the muslin, leaving a gap at the edges for the steam to come through. Fold over the edges of the muslin, place the lid on the steamer, and leave to steam for 20 minutes until the rice is tender but still firm.

4 Meanwhile, heat the coconut milk in a heavy pan with the sugar and a pinch of salt, stirring all the time until the sugar has dissolved. Stir in the steamed sticky rice until well mixed.

5 Remove from the heat, cover the pan and leave the rice to sit for 10–15 minutes until it has absorbed the sweetened coconut milk.

COOK'S TIP

In the north of Peninsular Malaysia, where much of the rice is grown and the influence from Thailand is strong, these banana leaf bundles are popular snacks. They are also in great demand at the Malay hawker stalls in the fast-paced cities of Kuala Lumpur and Singapore.

Per Portion Energy 232Kcal/981kJ; Protein 3.1g; Carbohydrate 55.1g, of which sugars 31g; Fat 0.6g, of which saturates 0.3g; Cholesterol 0mg; Calcium 46mg; Fibre 0.6g; Sodium 112mg.

DEEP-FRIED BANANAS WITH COCONUT

PERHAPS THE MOST COMMON OF ALL THE SWEET SNACKS, DEEP-FRIED BANANAS ARE POPULAR THROUGHOUT SOUTH-EAST ASIA, AND ARE A HAWKER-STALL FAVOURITE IN SINGAPORE. THEY ARE OFTEN EATEN ON THEIR OWN, SPRINKLED WITH SUGAR, OR THEY CAN BE SERVED WITH ICE CREAM.

SERVES FOUR TO SIX

INGREDIENTS
  115g/4oz/1 cup plain (all-purpose) or rice flour
  5ml/1 tsp baking powder
  2 eggs
  750ml/1¼ pints/3 cups coconut milk
  30ml/2 tbsp palm (jaggery) or granulated (white) sugar
  90g/3½oz fresh coconut, grated or desiccated (dry unsweetened shredded) coconut
  3 large bananas, halved widthways and lengthways
  vegetable oil, for deep-frying
  salt
  caster (superfine) or icing (confectioners') sugar, for sprinkling

1 Sift the flour with the baking powder and a pinch of salt into a bowl. Make a well in the centre and drop in the eggs. Gradually pour in the coconut milk, beating all the time, until the batter is thick and smooth.

2 Beat in the sugar and fresh dessicated coconut and add the banana pieces, coating each completely with the batter.

3 Heat enough oil for deep-frying in a wok or large heavy pan. Check the oil is the right temperature by dropping in a cube of bread – if it sizzles and turns golden brown, the oil is ready.

4 Lift the pieces of banana out of the batter with tongs or chopsticks and lower them into the oil. Fry two or three pieces at a time, until crisp and golden, and drain on kitchen paper. Repeat with the remaining banana pieces.

5 Sprinkle caster or icing sugar over the banana fritters and serve while they are still warm.

Per Portion Energy 377Kcal/1571kJ; Protein 5g; Carbohydrate 39.6g, of which sugars 22.7g; Fat 22.5g, of which saturates 9.9g; Cholesterol 63mg; Calcium 26mg; Fibre 3.2g; Sodium 30mg.

GLUTINOUS RICE WITH COCONUT

AT PERANAKAN WEDDINGS AND OTHER SPECIAL OCCASIONS, THIS DESSERT IS INVARIABLY FEATURED.
IT IS TRADITIONALLY WRAPPED IN BANANA LEAVES BUT THIS IS NOT NECESSARY IF YOU CANNOT
OBTAIN THESE. INSTEAD, MAKE IT IN A TRAY AND CUT IT INTO WEDGES TO SERVE.

3 Cut the pandan leaf into small pieces and distribute all over the tray, pushing a few pieces into the rice. Steam the rice for about 20 minutes. Check to see if it is cooked by tasting a few grains.

4 Put the palm sugar into a small pan and add the water. Stir over a gentle heat until all the sugar has dissolved, then remove from heat and blend with the coconut. Mix well.

5 Remove the rice from the steamer and press the desiccated coconut on top, spreading it evenly all over the surface of the rice. Cut into wedges to serve cold.

SERVES FOUR TO SIX

INGREDIENTS
    200g/7oz glutinous rice, soaked in
      water for 3 hours
    2.5ml/½ tsp salt
    1 pandan (screwpine) leaf
    125g/4¼oz palm sugar (jaggery)
    200ml/7fl oz/scant 1 cup water
    200g/7oz desiccated (dry
      unsweetened shredded) coconut

1 Drain the glutinous rice from the soaking water, rinse in a sieve (strainer) under running water and drain again.

2 Place in a bamboo steaming tray with enough water to moisten it and stir in the salt. There should be no surplus water as the rice will already have absorbed a sufficient amount for the steaming process.

Per portion Energy 457Kcal/1947kJ; Protein 8.6g; Carbohydrate 102.4g, of which sugars 50.8g; Fat 4.4g, of which saturates 1.3g; Cholesterol 0mg; Calcium 92mg; Fibre 0.5g; Sodium 381mg.

RED BEAN PUDDING

CHINESE IN ORIGIN BUT POPULAR THROUGHOUT SOUTH-EAST ASIA, TINY RED ADUKI BEANS ARE OFTEN SERVED AS A SWEET SNACK. RED, YELLOW AND GREEN BEANS ARE USED IN MANY CHINESE SWEET DISHES, SUCH AS THE SYRUPY SOUPS OR SPONGY DUMPLINGS FILLED WITH BEAN PASTE.

SERVES FOUR TO SIX

INGREDIENTS

115g/4oz dried red aduki beans, soaked in water for 2 hours
1.2 litres/2 pints/5 cups water
4 pandan (screwpine) leaves
150g/5oz/¾ cup sugar
150ml/¼ pint /⅔ cup thick coconut milk, fresh or canned, beaten until smooth, or fresh coconut cream

VARIATION

Generally, pandan leaves are used to flavour the syrup in this dish but you could easily use a flavouring of your choice, such as fresh root ginger, bay or lime leaves, lemon grass or vanilla.

1 Drain the soaked beans and put them in a deep pan. Add the water and bring it to the boil. Add the pandan leaves and reduce the heat. Simmer, uncovered, for about 40 minutes until the beans are tender and the water has greatly reduced. Stir in the sugar.

2 Allow the sugar to dissolve, and simmer for a further 10 minutes. Remove the pandan leaves and spoon the beans into individual bowls. Serve hot or leave to cool and chill before serving. Serve the coconut milk or cream separately, to pour over.

Per Portion Energy 155Kcal/661kJ; Protein 4.4g; Carbohydrate 35.8g, of which sugars 27.8g; Fat 0.4g, of which saturates 0.1g; Cholesterol 0mg; Calcium 40mg; Fibre 3g; Sodium 33mg.

CONDIMENTS

The essential condiments of South-east Asia add delicious textures and piquancy to many dishes. Although they are often thought of as aromatic spicy dips or side dishes, they are in fact more than optional extras, often imparting the heat or flavour that really makes the meal. Wonderfully simple to prepare, the dips, sambals and pickles in this chapter are exquisitely tasty and lift a feast of Singaporean dishes to memorable heights.

LIME PICKLE

THIS INDIAN PICKLE IS POPULAR AMONG THE INDIAN COMMUNITIES OF SINGAPORE. OFTEN SOLD IN JARS AT HAWKER STALLS, THE PICKLE IS EATEN MAINLY AS AN ACCOMPANIMENT TO FIERY CURRIES.

SERVES EIGHT TO TEN

INGREDIENTS
- 8–10 limes
- 30ml/2 tbsp salt
- 150ml/5fl oz/⅔ cup sesame or groundnut (peanut) oil
- 10–15ml/2–3 tsp brown mustard seeds
- 3–4 garlic cloves, cut into thin sticks
- 25g/1oz fresh root ginger, peeled and cut into thin sticks
- 5ml/1 tsp coriander seeds
- 5ml/1 tsp cumin seeds
- 5ml/1 tsp fennel seeds
- 10ml/2 tsp ground turmeric
- 10ml/2 tsp hot chilli powder or paste
- a handful of fresh or dried curry leaves

1 Put the whole limes in a bowl. Cover with boiling water and leave to stand for 30 minutes. Drain and cut into quarters. Rub the lime pieces with salt and put them into a sealed sterilized jar. Leave the limes to cure in the salt for 1 week.

2 Heat the oil in a wok and stir in the mustard seeds. When they begin to pop, stir in the garlic, ginger, spices and curry leaves. Cook gently for a few minutes to flavour the oil, then stir in the lime pieces and the juices from the jar. Reduce the heat and simmer the pickle for about 45 minutes, stirring from time to time.

3 Pour the pickle into sterilized jars and store in a cool place for 1–2 months.

COOK'S TIP
This pickle is delicious served with grilled (broiled) or fried fish, and spicy stir-fried noodles. You can make it as fiery as you like by adding more or less chilli powder.

Per Portion Energy 96Kcal/395kJ; Protein 0.3g; Carbohydrate 0.9g, of which sugars 0.6g; Fat 10.1g, of which saturates 1.5g; Cholesterol 0mg; Calcium 25mg; Fibre 0.2g; Sodium 1185mg.

SAMBAL SERONDENG

A QUINTESSENTIAL DRESSING FOR CURRIES IN SINGAPORE, SERONDENG ORIGINATED IN INDONESIA, WHERE IT WAS EATEN WITH A MOUTHWATERING MELANGE OF DISHES BUILT AROUND RICE.

SERVES SIX TO EIGHT

INGREDIENTS
    2 stalks lemon grass
    5 shallots
    4 garlic cloves
    3 fresh red chillies, seeded
      (optional)
    50g/2oz tempeh (fermented soy
      bean cake)
    30ml/2 tbsp vegetable or groundnut
      (peanut) oil
    175g/6oz fresh coconut, grated
      or 100g/3½oz desiccated
      (dry, unsweetened, shredded)
      coconut
    2.5ml/½ tsp salt
    2.5ml/½ tsp sugar

1 Trim the lemon grass stalks and slice the 7.5cm/3in at the root end into very thin rounds.

2 Peel and slice the shallots and the garlic. Slice the chillies diagonally into thin pieces.

3 Cut the tempeh into small dice, and fry it in oil in a wok or heavy pan until light brown. Crush it coarsely.

4 Heat another wok without oil and dry fry the lemon grass, shallots, garlic and chillies until just sizzled. Add the coconut, and stir-fry with a to and fro motion until all the ingredients are golden brown.

5 Add the crushed tempeh, salt and sugar and fry, stirring, until well-mixed. Remove from the heat and leave to cool before storing in an air-tight container, if not serving immediately. Keep the serondeng in the refrigerator and eat within a week.

COOK'S TIPS
Serondeng is delicious sprinkled over dishes like beef rendang, coconut milk kormas and curries or over plain rice as a relish. Use freshly grated coconut for the best flavour as store-bought desiccated coconut is over-dehydrated. Good serondeng should be succulent and softly moist.

Per portion Energy 120Kcal/494kJ; Protein 1.7g; Carbohydrate 4.1g, of which sugars 3.3g; Fat 10.8g, of which saturates 7g; Cholesterol 0mg; Calcium 44mg; Fibre 2.2g; Sodium 128mg.

LIME AND CHILLI DIP

FOR THIS DIP, IT IS BEST TO USE CALAMANSI LIMES, WHICH ARE INDIGENOUS TO SOUTH-EAST ASIA AND HAVE VERY THIN SKINS THAT CAN BE GRATED TO ADD TO THE SAUCE. WEST INDIAN LIMES CAN BE USED PROVIDED YOU GRATE THE SKIN THINLY, OTHERWISE THE SAUCE WILL HAVE A BITTER EDGE.

SERVES FOUR TO SIX

INGREDIENTS

    6 calamansi limes
    4 red chillies
    2 garlic cloves
    2 spring onions (scallions)
    2 kaffir lime leaves
    15ml/1 tbsp fish sauce
    5ml/1 tsp sugar
    30ml/2 tbsp water

1 Finely grate the rind of one lime into a bowl. Squeeze the juice from all the limes into the bowl and, with a spoon, scoop out the flesh. Discard the seeds.

2 Finely chop the chillies, garlic and spring onions. Shred the lime leaves finely. Mix these ingredients into the lime juice and add the sugar, fish sauce and water. Stir everything together.

3 Taste and adjust the proportions if necessary, adding more water or lime juice as needed. Serve the dip with fish and chicken dishes or salads.

Per portion Energy 9Kcal/38kJ; Protein 0.6g; Carbohydrate 1.6g, of which sugars 1.3g; Fat 0.1g, of which saturates 0g; Cholesterol 0mg; Calcium 6mg; Fibre 0.1g; Sodium 179mg.

CHILLI, GARLIC AND GINGER SAUCE

REGARDED AS THE HOLY TRINITY OF SPICES, CHILLIES, GARLIC AND GINGER HAVE AN EXTRAORDINARY AFFINITY WHEN THEY ARE COMBINED IN THE CORRECT PROPORTIONS. THE CHILLIES MUST BE ABSOLUTELY FRESH. THE GARLIC SHOULD BE FRESH AND PLUMP WITH NO WRINKLY SKINS.

MAKES ABOUT 300ML/½ PINT/1½ CUPS

INGREDIENTS

10 fresh red chillies
10 cloves garlic
50g/2oz fresh root ginger
200ml/7fl oz/scant 1 cup rice
  wine vinegar
2.5ml/½ tsp salt
30ml/2 tbsp vegetable oil
2 spring onions (scallions)
2.5ml/½ tsp sugar

1 Wash the chillies and pat them dry. It is important that you do not introduce moisture into the sauce as it will encourage bacterial growth and the sauce will not keep well. Do not remove the seeds of the chillies in this case as the sauce is intended to give sweet, sharp fire to dishes. Chop roughly.

2 Peel the garlic and wipe dry with kitchen paper: do not wash it. Chop the flesh roughly.

3 With a sharp paring knife, peel or scrape off the thin outer skin of the ginger. If the roots you are using have any green stems attached, do not discard these. Roughly chop the ginger.

COOK'S TIP
When ready to eat, scoop out as much as is needed with a clean dry spoon and add more rice wine vinegar and sugar to the sauce to taste.

4 Place all three ingredients in a mortar and pestle or food processor and process until fine, but be careful not to reduce it to a purée consistency. To facilitate the grinding, add a spoonful or two of the vinegar.

5 Turn the mixture into a bowl and combine with the remaining vinegar and the salt. Heat the oil in a small pan or wok and add to the sauce. Finely chop the spring onions and mix them in well. Keep in a jar with a screw-top lid.

Per quantity Energy 339Kcal/1405kJ; Protein 13.9g; Carbohydrate 18.1g, of which sugars 3.5g; Fat 23.9g, of which saturates 2.7g; Cholesterol 0mg; Calcium 100mg; Fibre 4.6g; Sodium 1070mg.

GINGER AND GARLIC SALT

THIS IS A CLASSIC DIP FOR CANTONESE DEEP-FRIED CHICKEN. IT IS VERY EASY TO MAKE. IF YOU CAN FIND COARSE-GRAINED SEA SALT, IT IS IDEAL FOR THIS MIXTURE, AS IT HAS A FULLER FLAVOUR AND AN APPETIZINGLY FLAKY TEXTURE, AS WELL AS A LOWER SODIUM CONTENT.

MAKES ENOUGH AS A DIP FOR 1 CHICKEN

INGREDIENTS
  50g/2oz fresh root ginger, peeled
  4 garlic cloves
  30ml/2 tbsp vegetable oil
  15ml/1 tbsp sesame oil
  2.5ml/½ tsp sugar
  5ml/1 tsp salt
  2.5ml/½ tsp freshly ground
    black pepper
  1 spring onion (scallion)

COOK'S TIP
If you don't have a microwave, heat the mixture in a small pan for 2 minutes.

1 Grate the ginger and finely chop the garlic. Blend in a small bowl and mix in the oils, sugar, salt and pepper. Microwave for 1 minute to cook the oil so the sauce will not have a raw taste.

2 Chop the spring onion very finely and stir it into the sauce. Leave the sauce to cool and store it in a jar with a screw top, in the refrigerator, if you are not using it immediately.

Per quantity Energy 401Kcal/1650kJ; Protein 0.5g; Carbohydrate 0.8g, of which sugars 0.7g; Fat 44.1g, of which saturates 5.8g; Cholesterol 0mg; Calcium 27mg; Fibre 0.7g; Sodium 1996mg.

DRIED SHRIMP AND CHILLI CONDIMENT

LOOK FOR DRIED SHRIMPS THAT ARE LARGE, UNBROKEN AND A DULL PINKISH BROWN. THEY ARE MUCH EASIER TO PROCESS WHEN SOAKED BRIEFLY IN WARM WATER UNTIL JUST SOFT BUT NOT MUSHY. DRAIN THEM TO REMOVE ANY DUST, WHICH IS INVARIABLY PRESENT.

SERVES FOUR

INGREDIENTS
    2 spring onions (scallions)
    50g/2oz dried shrimps
    6 shallots
    4 garlic cloves
    30ml/2 tbsp water
    30ml/2 tbsp lime juice
    5ml/1 tsp sugar

1 Hold the spring onions by their green tops and run the white parts briefly over a gas flame until they are lightly charred and frizzled. Trim and cut into short lengths.

2 Peel and slice the garlic and shallots. Grind them together with the spring onions in a mortar and pestle or a food processor to a coarse paste.

3 Remove the paste to a bowl, then grind the soaked dried shrimps finely. Add them to the bowl and mix all the ingredients together thoroughly.

4 Add the lime juice, sugar and water and blend well.

Per portion Energy 59kcal/247kJ; Protein 8.1g; Carbohydrate 6g, of which sugars 4.1g; Fat 0.5g, of which saturates 0.1g; Cholesterol 63mg; Calcium 166mg; Fibre 1g; Sodium 543mg.

INDEX